THE EMERGENCE OF AFRICAN CAPITALISM

THE EMERGENCE OF AFRICAN CAPITALISM

John Iliffe

The Anstey Memorial Lectures
in the University of Kent at Canterbury
10–13 May 1982

University of Minnesota Press, Minneapolis

338.04
J28e

221996

Library of Congress Cataloging in Publication Data

Iliffe, John.
   The Emergence of African Capitalism.

   "The Anstey memorial lectures in the University of
Kent at Canterbury, 10–13 May 1982."
   Bibliography: p.
   Includes index.
   1. Africa, Sub-Saharan—Economic conditions.
2. Capitalists and financiers—Africa, Sub-Saharan—
History.   I. Title.
HC800.I44   1983   338'.04'0967   83–5922
ISBN 0–8166–1236–6
ISBN 0–8166–1237–4 (pbk.)

Contents

Acknowledgements

This book is an expanded version of the Anstey Memorial Lectures given in the University of Kent at Canterbury in May 1982. I wish to thank the community of historians at Canterbury for inviting me to deliver the lectures. I am also grateful to them and to the Master and members of Eliot College for the friendliness of their welcome and the generosity of their hospitality.

In preparing the lectures I made reconnaissance trips (and nothing more) to Kano, Nairobi, and Abidjan. In Kano I was indebted to Lorne Larson and to the authorities of Bayero University, who kindly granted me research association. In Nairobi I was helped by Peter Kinyanjui and the librarians of the Institute of Development Studies. Henry Bernstein, David Birmingham, David Fieldhouse, Jack Goody, John Lonsdale, Sandy Robertson, and members of the audience at Canterbury made helpful comments on the lectures. Sandy Robertson let me see some of his work before publication. I am grateful to all those who have helped me.

St John's College, Cambridge   John Iliffe
May 1982

Foreword

The Anstey Memorial Lectures were established in 1982 to honour Roger Anstey who was the first Professor of Modern History in the University of Kent at Canterbury. In the ten years preceding his premature death Roger Anstey made a characteristically many-sided contribution to the Kent school of history which included a special interest in African and Caribbean studies. The experience on which he built his career came from two fields. The first was colonial history in which he published two major works on the history of the Zaire region of Central Africa, including a detailed study of Belgian rule in the Congo. This experience was broadened by several years of teaching at Ibadan, a leading Nigerian university. The second half of Anstey's academic career was devoted to studies in the slave trade. His wide-ranging interests extended into analyses of religious, political, economic and even quantitative history, all fields which could be explored in future memorial lectures. The scholarly path which Roger Anstey pursued with dedication, both at the University of Durham and at Kent, culminated brilliantly in *The Atlantic Slave Trade and British Abolition 1760–1810*. Shortly before his death in 1979 he convened an international conference on Anti-Slavery, Religion and Reform, the proceedings of which were published by Christine Bolt and Seymour Drescher together with an appreciation of Roger Anstey by David Brion Davis. It seemed fitting that this career of outstanding scholarship should be commemorated by a biannual series of published memorial lectures. The University of Kent is indebted to John Iliffe of St John's College, Cambridge, for giving the first series of Anstey Memorial Lectures.

David Birmingham
Professor of Modern History
University of Kent at Canterbury

1 An Indigenous Capitalism?

Roger Anstey's major work was on the abolition of the Atlantic slave trade.[1] He chose to study one of the most contentious issues in modern history, an issue still capable of arousing powerful emotions. Through the contention and the controversy he took a narrow, winding, subtle path, seeking to weigh and connect the elements of abstract principle, national interest, personal advantage, and political skill which together brought about the abolition of the slave trade. Anstey's path was specifically a historian's path. His contribution was specifically a historian's contribution. As a member of the College of Wilberforce and Clarkson, and as a man so close in spirit to them, it was fitting that he should have been their historian. I am a member of the same College and I am honoured to have been invited to give these first lectures in his memory.

But Roger Anstey was also, and first, a historian of Africa,[2] and in these lectures I hope to follow his lead through a minefield of African controversy. Since the industrial revolution men have debated whether capitalism, having transformed the West, can also develop non-Western societies. Characteristically, it was Marx who gave the issue its modern shape in the articles on British rule in India which he wrote for the *New York Daily Tribune* in 1853, where he argued that Western capitalism was bringing about 'a fundamental revolution in the social state of Asia'.[3] As he grew older, however, Marx also grew more impressed by the capacity of Asian societies to resist capitalism.[4] Later, between the wars, the Comintern repeatedly debated whether indigenous capitalists could be a progressive force in colonial and semi-colonial societies. After 1945 the failure of Latin America's orthodox communist parties and the success of Castro's insurrection gave weight to the views of the dependency theorists, who argued that the peripheral capitalism which Latin America had experienced had brought not development but underdevelopment. This view, predominant on the left for thirty years, itself came under attack during the 1970s. One of its critics has recently urged us to 'rid ourselves of the ideological handicap of dependency theory'.[5]

In Africa the question is not merely theoretical. It is a matter of practical action. Should young Africans work with or against political movements whose purpose is to create national capitalism? Is national capitalism feasible? Is it desirable? Or is President Nyerere right to argue that an autonomous national capitalism is impossible in Africa and that socialism is therefore 'the rational choice'?[6] During the last twenty years most young Africans would have had little hesitation: they would have agreed with Nyerere. Perhaps they still would, but I am not sure that they would still be quite so confident. Meanwhile the same question has engaged many of the best minds in African studies and provoked perhaps the liveliest recent debate in the field, some demonstrating that no true capitalism has yet come into being,[7] while others describe the emergence of national bourgeoisies.[8] At the same time a wider public is becoming aware that rich and dynamic African businessmen do exist: Chief Alhaji Yinka Folawiyo, whose private shipping company, Nigerian Green Lines, was reported in 1979 to own six cargo carriers – a total of 87,807 tons deadweight – operating between Nigeria and continental Europe;[9] or Kenya's Assistant Minister of Commerce and Industry, Njenga Karume, who in 1974 was a director of 36 firms, had a financial stake in 33 of them, and had founded a shoe-manufacturing company which aspired to challenge multinational domination of the Kenyan market;[10] or the Senegalese trader and transporter, Alhaji Momar Sourang, who was prominent in his country's ruling party and in the powerful Islamic brotherhood known as the Mourides, and was Secretary-General of the World Islamic Chamber of Commerce;[11] or the Dantata family of Kano in northern Nigeria, who are now possibly the wealthiest merchants and industrialists in tropical Africa but whose founder lived in a house 'rendered almost uninhabitable . . . by the untidy stacks of files which encroached everywhere on the living space' and was said never to have stopped work 'except at the times for prayer'.[12] Meanwhile other Africans – not businessmen but politicians, publicists, intellectuals – are beginning to articulate a specifically capitalist ethic. The most outspoken is probably Kenya's Minister of Constitutional Affairs, Charles Njonjo, as he is reported to have told Kenya's parliament in May 1981:

Njonjo: I am a capitalist. I believe in African socialism . . . I have got a three-piece suit! Does it not explain what I am?
Hon. Members: Hear! Hear! Hear!
Njonjo: . . . Sir, I do not believe that this nation will be served by paupers![13]

As a historian I am not primarily concerned with whether capitalism can be established in Africa, either in theory or in the future. Nor am I concerned with whether it would be desirable if it were. I am concerned with whether and how far it has actually come into being: that is, how far black capitalists have come into being and established their predominance. I am concerned with when and where and why and how this may have happened. I am concerned with what men thought about it and how they responded to it. And I am concerned especially with whether the capitalism that may have come into being in Africa may in some way have been distinctive in a global comparison, for I suspect that this is a subject where African experience, because it is recent and well-documented, may illuminate the history of other continents. I am not suggesting that there is some unique form of African Capitalism comparable to that mythical creature, African Socialism, which so many explorers hunted fruitlessly in the 1960s. By capitalism I mean the classic, essentially Marxian definition: the production of goods for exchange by capitalists who combine capital and land which they own with labour power which they buy from free and propertyless workers. Capitalism, in my usage, centres on the exploitation of the labour power of free wage-labourers, for, as Marx wrote of capitalism late in his life, 'The relation between capital and wage-labour determines the entire character of the mode of production.'[14] Moreover, from the viewpoint of a working historian, the wage relationship is the aspect of capitalism which can be traced with greatest precision in the records of the past; it is, for example, the chief analytical tool used in the two classic studies of European capitalism, Lenin's account of Russia and Maurice Dobb's history of capitalism in Britain.[15] It is true, of course, that some wage-labour can exist where other modes of production are dominant, and I shall mention African examples later in this lecture. But such wage-labour normally exists in antagonism to the other modes, and where the relationship between capitalists and wage-labourers exists as the dominant and self-reproducing relation of production, that is capitalism.

At its core, then, African capitalism is by definition identical to capitalism elsewhere. But surrounding the core, the flesh may have distinctive shapes and qualities. This was the question that interested Max Weber about European capitalism: its differences from capitalism elsewhere and the reasons for them, which he believed to lie in Calvinism.[16] Maxime Rodinson asked the same question about capitalism in the Islamic world, although it is salutary that he concluded 'There has been no special Muslim road for capitalism.'[17]

These lectures, then, are about the existence, the history, and the distinctiveness of African capitalism. I shall argue that it has indeed been distinctive and that its special qualities result, on the one hand, from the very late stage in the global history of capitalism at which that system of production developed in Africa, and, on the other hand, from the special characteristics of Africa's pre-capitalist societies. It is, of course, a huge subject, much of it still unexplored, but, as my favourite African proverb says, 'He who waits for the whole animal to appear, spears the tail.'

The starting-point is sub-Saharan Africa in the mid-nineteenth century on the eve of European conquest. Were there in the sub-continent at that time any extensive capitalist relationships, any growth points of an indigenous capitalism? If we look across sub-Saharan Africa with that question in mind, a broad distinction emerges between those regions which were already substantially linked to the outside world by trade or other economic ties and those which were not. Of the five regions linked to the larger world, that with the longest contact was the savanna region of West Africa, whose ties were across the Sahara with North Africa and the Middle East. North of the Sahara the dominant economic pattern of the Islamic world was the coexistence of merchant capitalism in the sphere of exchange with pre-capitalist modes of production: the existence of what Rodinson called a 'capitalistic sector' of exchange amidst peasants and craftsmen who still owned the means of production.[18] Long before the nineteenth century this capitalistic sector had extended into the savanna region of West Africa through the dispersal of North African and Saharan merchants along the desert trade routes. So much did the savanna belong to the larger world that when, after nearly two years of travel, the first European reached Kano, the region's main commercial centre, and passed through the gates of the city on 20 January 1824, nobody paid the slightest attention to him.[19] By the end of the nineteenth century one or two African merchants based in the savanna had reversed the commercial relationship with the north by employing their own agents on the North African coast: the best known was probably Malam Yaroh, the leading African merchant of Zinder, in modern Niger, during the last quarter of the nineteenth century.[20] The commercial mechanisms which Malam Yaroh and the other merchants of the savanna used were mainly of Middle Eastern origin: Arabic weights and measures; currencies of cowrie shells and silver originally imported from North Africa; and

Islamic systems of credit and commercial paper, together with Islamic devices for evading Koranic restrictions on interest.[21] When Kano's first European visitor eventually made himself known, he was offered cash in return for a bill on the British Consul in Tripoli.[22] African merchants moved funds around in the same way by means of commercial paper. Malam Yaroh, for example, accepted goods in Zinder in return for bills on his branch in Kano.[23] There were distinctive features to savanna trade, but the framework was that which was common to the Islamic world.

Yet if a capitalistic sector of exchange existed in the West African savanna in the nineteenth century, did capitalist production exist? For Marx pointed out that merchant capital could coexist with almost any system of production. He doubted, indeed, whether merchant capital could of itself change an existing production system, and certainly it could not do so unless it 'took root' within that system and transformed it from within.[24] In the West African savanna pre-capitalist modes of production were dominant and several coexisted: domestic production by the family unit, in which the main form of exploitation was by senior men of their juniors and womenfolk; domestic production by cultivators or craftsmen within a political state which extracted surplus through tribute; and the very widespread use of slaves, especially in the vicinity of the major trading centres. This diversity of pre-capitalist modes of production was to be one of the keys to African capitalism in the twentieth century. But the immediate question is whether there were any nuclei of capitalist production amidst the dominant pre-capitalist modes of the nineteenth century.

As usual, the place to begin is to look for hired labour. Three kinds existed in the West African savanna during the nineteenth century. First, there are very rare and seemingly random references to free men working as hired agricultural labourers. On his epic walk from Guinea to Timbuktu in 1827, René Caillié noticed at Tiémé, in the northwest of modern Ivory Coast, a cultivator who lacked slaves and therefore 'had several free Bambaras at work for him. . . . When they had done work, I observed that [he] paid his labourers in kind.'[25] The townsmen of Jenne – on an island in the Niger in modern Mali – employed small numbers of seasonal agricultural labourers during the late nineteenth century, paying them in cowrie shells, as did farm-owners in parts of Hausaland, according to oral traditions from northern Nigeria.[26] An element of hired labour within pre-capitalist class societies has been very common historically; in Europe it is at least as old as Homer.[27] Occasional references in West Africa are therefore not surprising. The significant point is probably their rarity.

Much more common was the use of hired workers as porters. Philip Curtin's research among the Jahaanke traders of Bundu in Senegal found that they 'are unanimous and strong in their insistence that their ancestors used hired porters, not slaves or free men recruited through kinship ties, for their commercial ventures to the kola regions'.[28] The Dyula traders who linked together the western savanna and the forest used hired porters alongside slaves and kinsmen, paying them a tenth of what they carried, while the first French officers stationed in the Gyaman kingdom in modern Ivory Coast reported that porterage was the only form of paid labour there. In Hausaland hired porters were employed on the route from Kano to Adamawa and were also used for the transport of building materials within Kano city.[29] It is probably true that no substantial number of professional, full-time porters existed in West Africa until the end of the nineteenth century,[30] but the evidence of seasonal porterage for hire is extensive and it raises the question why hired labour should have been most common in caravan porterage. A major reason may have been that the demand for labour was too irregular to be met economically by slaves and too large to be met by kinsmen. In addition, porterage was closely entwined with the monetised trading system. It was perhaps a particularly despised and arduous task of the kind which a pre-capitalist society often relegates to casual wage-labourers who are regarded as socially inferior even to slaves. And porterage was a task where the control and measurement of the labour performed was particularly easy.[31] Whatever the reason, human transport was usually the first form of hired labour in sub-Saharan Africa.

But perhaps the most interesting possibility is that in the West African savanna – and only there – a third form of paid labour may have existed, in craft industry. It would have been only one of several forms of craft production. In certain savanna towns entrepreneurs employed slaves as domestic textile workers; this is best documented for Sinsani, a town on the Niger in modern Mali, and elsewhere in Mali, among the Soninke people, weaving is still monopolised by men of slave ancestry.[32] More commonly craft producers were free men working as small domestic groups. In the western savanna they frequently belonged to closed castes of low status. Our best evidence of such an industrial system comes from Jenne, where at the beginning of this century a French officer, Charles Monteil, wrote a detailed account of the town's economy shortly after European conquest.[33] The predominant form of craft industry in Jenne was domestic artisan production in its purest form. 'In reality', Monteil explained, 'the artisan produces only to commission [*sur commande*]. He then obtains, on credit, the materials indispensable to his work and repays the cost with the majority of his earnings.'[34] The arrangement was simplest in classic artisan occupations like leatherworking, but it extended also to the building of houses and boats, where craftsmen expected all materials to be supplied while they themselves provided only labour for which they were paid by the day in cowries. Even the rural migrants who came into the town to work as weavers were normally paid by the task or the commission; only exceptionally, Monteil wrote, did they hire themselves out on other terms, and this is the only indication in his account that anything other than the simplest form of domestic artisan production existed in Jenne. Clearly commercial capitalism had made almost no impact on domestic industry there.

At almost the same time as Monteil was compiling his account of Jenne, a similar description was being written of the Hausa region of the central Sudan which is today the core of northern Nigeria. It was written by a Hausa cleric, Imam Imoru, and it is probably the most valuable account we have of the West African savanna in the nineteenth century.[35] With regard to industrial production, Hausaland differed from Jenne in three ways. First, its craftsmen did not belong to castes, although they were normally hereditary. Second, in the nineteenth century Hausaland was a vastly more important producer. In particular, Kano's production of indigo-dyed cotton cloth was the most important craft industry in sub-Saharan Africa; Kano clothed half the central Sudan, so it was said in the 1890s, and its cloth could be bought everywhere from Alexandria to Lagos and was exported to Brazil.[36] The third point of distinction was that Kano's cloth production was mainly a rural industry rooted in the small towns and dense agricultural population of the Kano Emirate, 'one of the most fertile spots on earth' according to Heinrich Barth in the mid-nineteenth century.[37] Cloth output had grown greatly from the seventeenth century as a result of a shift in Saharan trading patterns from the western to the central savanna, the formation of a single monetised trading zone throughout the central savanna in the eighteenth century, and the creation of a single political unit covering the same area – the Sokoto Caliphate – at the beginning of the nineteenth century.[38] These together made Kano the predominant textile centre of West Africa. It was especially famous for its indigo-dyed cloth. The dyeing process was in two stages. First the cloth was soaked in an indigo solution in large dyepits, a particularly evil-smelling operation. Then it was taken to teams of beaters who used wooden mallets to beat powdered indigo into the fabric until it had the glossy, almost black sheen which made the finest cloth, Yan Kura, so distinctive. 'The sound of the mallets beaten in rhythm fills certain streets in Kano and Kura', wrote an early observer, 'and gives the impression, very rarely met in the native towns, of a genuine industrial activity.'[39] A dyed and beaten cloth could cost twice as much as an unfinished one.

Yet the interesting point about Imam Imoru's account of craft production in Hausaland is that, apart from the absence of castes, it is almost identical to Monteil's account of Jenne, despite the great differences between the two areas. In Imam Imoru's account, Hausa craftsmen worked for clients, not for wages. 'If a man has yarn to dye', he explains, 'he gives the dyer cowrie shells to dye it for him.'[40] If we were to believe the written sources, there would be no significant evidence that merchant capital penetrated craft production in the West African savanna in the nineteenth century. There would be no evidence of putting-out systems, where a merchant rather than the craftsman or his customer owned the working capital. Nor would there be evidence of entrepreneurs owning fixed capital – looms or dyepits, for example – and paying wages to those who worked them. There is no significant written evidence from the nineteenth-century West African savanna of any trend towards what in Europe is now called proto-industrialisation.

Recently, however, historians have begun to investigate the oral sources for the economic history of the savanna, especially Hausaland, and they have begun to reveal a different picture. The most important work has been Dr Philip Shea's study of the craftsmen and merchants who made and sold Yan Kura.[41] Their modern successors told Dr Shea that during the nineteenth century Kano's cloth merchants began to buy unfinished cloth from the weavers and put it out for processing by dyers and beaters in return for what was in effect a wage. The merchant then received the cloth back for marketing; his signature on the bale acted as a trademark. Recent research elsewhere in the central savanna suggests that putting-out systems of this kind were quite common there.[42] A Nigérien scholar, André Salifou, has described (perhaps with some exaggeration) the organisation which Malam Yaroh of Zinder operated in the late nineteenth century:

Malam Yaroh had practically mobilised in his service the greater part of the peasants and artisans of Zinder and its environs. . . . He supplied them with the raw material and received in return the finished products: bands of cotton, basket-work, tanned skins . . . which he undertook to place, naturally to his profit, on the important market of the Maghreb. This rural labour was paid according to the importance of the work, sometimes in cowries but more often in kind: cloths, textiles from North Africa, trinkets.[43]

In Kano, however, Dr Shea learned that capitalist penetration of craft industry went beyond control of unfinished products to ownership of fixed capital. As the market grew during the nineteenth century, the dyeing process was simplified and a larger and more expensive kind of dyepit came into use. Many, although by no means all, of the new dyepits were established by cloth merchants, who began to hire cheap migrant labourers – often Koran school pupils – to perform the routine tasks. This further reduced production costs, so that the real price of Kano's cloth fell throughout the second half of the century, thereby still further expanding its market. By the late 1880s, if not before, Kano's cloth could outsell locally woven textiles even in what is now north-eastern Ghana, 600 miles away in a direct line.[44] It is striking, however, that the merchants were never able to penetrate the cloth-beating trade, for the beaters were highly skilled men – an untrained man can scarcely lift a cloth-beater's mallet – and they worked in small, tight-knit, co-operative groups which retained control of their occupation into the twentieth century.

Thus with respect to craft production in nineteenth-century Hausaland there is a flat contradiction between the written and oral evidence, a contradiction accentuated by the fact that Dr Shea did not use Imam Imoru's material. One important check, as Dr Shea himself suggests, would be to investigate the textile industry of Sokoto, the closest rival to Kano. In comparative terms there is much to be said for the picture which emerges from the oral sources. Kano's nineteenth-century textile production had expanded to such a totally different scale from Jenne's craft industry that it would have been strange if industrial organisation had not changed to meet the expansion. It is striking, too, that the evidence of capitalist organisation should come from the finishing branches of the trade, for in imperial China, where domestic spinning and weaving remained predominant as late as 1880, dyeing and calendering (a process similar to beating) came under capitalist control at a much earlier date, because in these branches substantial economies of scale were possible.[45] Much research remains to be done, but it is possible that Dr Shea and his fellows have revealed in the central Sudan a more advanced form of capitalism than has previously been suspected in pre-colonial Africa.

Nevertheless, even in Hausaland there were severe constraints on the further advance of capitalism. Even the wage-earners identified by Dr Shea in the dyeing industry were no more than seasonal migrants; there is no indication that they had lost their means of agricultural production. Throughout the savanna, land was too easily available to permit the intensive exploitation of free cultivators, so that the impact of merchant capital on agriculture was confined to marketing and the widespread ownership of slaves by rich merchants (who are sometimes said to have treated them more harshly than aristocrats did). The easier availability of slaves in the nineteenth century, which was an unintended consequence of the abolition of the overseas slave trade, may even have retarded the growth of capitalism; Dr Lovejoy has suggested that what distinguished slavery in Hausaland from that in Zanzibar or the Americas was the very weakness of market forces in the West African case.[46] Moreover, although the traders of the savanna enjoyed greater freedom from political control than did those of the West African forest – indeed, the savanna would meet one of the fundamental criteria which Needham and Wallerstein have seen as essential to the development of capitalism: an economy too large for any single

political authority to control[47] – nevertheless political constraints on capitalist ambition remained strong. Even in
Hausaland merchants needed aristocratic patrons and much of
their wealth was probably invested in loans to aristocrats.
Heavy death duties were exacted from officials there and
possibly also from wealthy merchants.[48] Partible inheritance
under Islamic law, accentuated by widespread polygyny,
tended to disperse property at death and prevent the
emergence of firms which could outlive their founders.[49] In
the phrase which Clifford Geertz applied to Indonesia, the
capitalism of the West African savanna in the nineteenth
century was 'bazaar capitalism', small in scale, commercial in
form, individualistic and ephemeral in organisation, with all
the stages in the production of an article generally performed
by one producer.[50]

These constraints on the growth of an indigenous capitalism
were even stronger in the second region of sub-Saharan Africa
which was linked to the world economy: the West African coast
and forest. Here the link was more recent than in the savanna,
dating at the earliest to the fifteenth century, and it was also
less direct, in the sense that the foreign traders were not
allowed to penetrate beyond the coast, so that trade with the
forest regions was conducted mainly by coastal middlemen. As
in the savanna, a capitalistic sector of exchange was combined
with several pre-capitalist modes of production, but it had
penetrated them less and had met stronger resistance.

To illustrate these points it is best to examine one area of
especially vigorous economic activity – the Gold Coast and its
hinterland, which today make up Ghana – and to look once
more for free wage-labour as against other means of
exploitation. In 1600 or thereabouts a Dutch visitor to the Gold
Coast reported that 'here there are no labourers to be found to
serve people for hire and reward, but only slaves and
captives'.[51] Even in the mid-nineteenth century the Gold
Coast's leading African merchants were those who most
successfully combined economic activity of a capitalist kind
with social relationships in an older style: men like George

Blankson, the 'commercial king', who was able 'to build a castle in his own town of Anomabu, wonderful to behold, and to support 100 slaves as servants of the palatial building', despite the fact that he was also a Legislative Councillor and Methodist lay preacher.[52] Such pre-capitalist relationships were essential because in the mid-nineteenth century regular wage-labourers were available only in the main coastal towns; hired agricultural workers simply did not exist.[53] The one occupation outside the towns for which men could be hired was, predictably, porterage; by the early seventeenth century this was already 'a respectable vocation keenly competed for by the able-bodied men'.[54]

Inland of the Gold Coast lay Asante, the most opulent and powerful of the West African forest states and, thanks to the work of Ivor Wilks, the best-known.[55] Wilks and his pupils have only begun to publish their work on the economic history of Asante, so that much remains obscure, but the main outlines are beginning to emerge. Nineteenth-century Asante was a highly commercialised society. Gold-dust acted as a general-purpose currency which could be lent at interest. Internal trade was conducted by itinerant pedlars and hawkers. Long-distance commerce was shared between state merchants and wealthy private traders. The private traders did not, however, become a wholly independent bourgeoisie. One reason was that slavery remained the predominant form of exploitation and wealthy men invested above all in people. Another was that Asante admired wealth and rewarded public-spirited generosity with offices and titles, culminating in the rich man's highest accolade, the golden elephant's tail. And thirdly, the state both harassed the wealthy commoner with unpredictable exactions while he was alive and claimed a large proportion of his self-acquired movable property when he died. As in imperial China, Asante's polity was a decisive constraint on the evolution of an indigenous capitalism. Early in the twentieth century a petitioner was to protest that death duties in particular had 'brought the downfall of the Ashanti nation and for this reason people had to bury their money under ground so that more money was hidden under ground than that on the earth'.[56] The consequence may be seen in the slender development of wage-labour. As so often, Asante traders frequently used hired porters,[57] but there is no evidence that merchant capital penetrated craft industry, although remarkably little is known about this.[58] Wilks has recently mentioned elements of landlordship and sharecropping in the vicinity of the capital and has promised further work on 'the beginnings of rural capitalism, and the development of a system of métayage [sharecropping] controlled by wealthy office-holders and others in the towns'.[59] Yet whatever this further work may show, it is clear that slavery and social and political constraints were even more effective in Asante than in the savanna in checking the emergence of capitalist production. That was probably equally true of other major forest peoples of the nineteenth century such as the Fon of Dahomey or the Yoruba of Nigeria, although we have as yet no study of the growth of capitalism in Yorubaland or in many other major African societies – a most important and exciting field for research.

The use of hired labour forms a simpler pattern when we move south into equatorial Africa, where a third area of the sub-continent – modern Angola and neighbouring regions – had been linked to the world economy since the arrival of Portuguese traders in the fifteenth century. In mid-nineteenth-century Angola the employment of hired labour by Africans appears to have been confined to caravan porters. The Ovimbundu ivory traders who were among Angola's leading entrepreneurs in this period operated their caravans, so it is said, 'through paid agents, officers, scouts, soldiers, "book-keepers", porters and slaves. The wages were paid in the form of European products or, in the case of high-ranking employees, by conceding them the right to carry along their own merchandise with the caravan.'[60] By contrast, Professor Birmingham has shown that when Brazilian, Portuguese, and African planters began to grow coffee in the Cazengo region from the 1830s, they were unable to recruit free workers and relied instead on slaves, long after slavery had theoretically become illegal.[61]

This pattern was repeated in eastern Africa, the fourth region linked to the world economy. Until the early nineteenth century its external contacts had been confined to the coast, except in Ethiopia in the north and Mozambique in the south where long-distance trade with the interior had developed earlier. In the mid-nineteenth century, wage-labour, whether rewarded in kind or cash, was confined almost entirely to the coast and the trading caravans. Hired porters were employed not only by Arab traders and European travellers but by some African traders based in the interior. The traditions of the Kamba people of Kenya, for example, suggest – perhaps with some exaggeration – that labour relations in long-distance trade passed from communal labour groups, through the employment of kin in return for food, to a 'hired cadre of caravan porter-workers' who were not necessarily kin and were paid in cattle and trade goods, the last stage being reached in the early nineteenth century.[62] Strikes by caravan porters for higher pay were common. On the coast itself slavery was the normal form of dependent labour but Zanzibar Island also had a number of free labourers and caravan porters awaiting employment who commonly undertook casual work for pay.[63]

In the interior of eastern Africa the evidence is more slender. There are scattered references to migrant labour by groups in special hardship.[64] Michael Cowen's research among the Kikuyu has revealed varied means by which wealthy men appropriated the labour power of their juniors: taking them into the household as herdsmen paid in stock, inducing them to cultivate in return for land and the payment of their bridewealth, or paying them in kind for clearing land on piece-rate terms. Cowen emphasises that all these procedures fell short of wage-labour because of the absence of money as a universal equivalent, while all but the last were remunerated in commodities which could reproduce the means of production rather than the means of subsistence, but he stresses the real continuity between these systems and later wage-labour.[65]

It is in the major states of eastern Africa that evidence of the emergence of wage relationships is most lacking. In Ethiopia, for example, trade was despised and was dominated by foreigners, crafts were performed by low-status caste groups, land was amply available, coins were rare, and wage relationships were largely confined to Tigre in the north – where contact with the outside world was greatest – until money became more common in the mid-nineteenth century and wages began to supplement the predominant relationships of clientage and slavery.[66] In the interlacustrine region the absence of hired labour was even more striking. In Buganda, for example, despite the existence of a cowrie currency and considerable long-distance trade from the early 1850s, all dependent labour was provided by women, slaves, and political clients until European missionaries began to pay for services. As a missionary explained in 1882, this was a dramatic innovation:

> The Natives are beginning to understand the meaning of working for hire. . . . Women have come forward and commenced to hoe and prune for cowries; while many lads . . . have gone so far as to break the custom of the country, and hoe for us every morning. It must be remembered that this is the work of women exclusively.[67]

Three years later, however, Buganda's pre-capitalist order reacted against this innovation and the missionaries were told 'to employ no Baganda or other natives as servants unless we buy them as slaves'.[68] In the Lozi kingdom of modern Zambia, similarly, the king urged pioneer missionaries not to create a precedent by paying for services.[69]

Thus in both western and eastern Africa in the nineteenth century, wage-labour and other indices of an emergent African capitalism were almost entirely confined to exchange, transport, and, possibly, craft production. Dependent agricultural labour, by contrast, was supplied by junior family members, political clients, or slaves. It is when we turn to

South Africa that this pattern is reversed. Here the external stimulus of trade with European settlements at the Cape was reinforced by the model of European farming and, above all, by deliberate missionary schemes to create Christian communities of African yeomen farmers and provide the protection against traditional society which they needed in order to flourish. Colin Bundy and Norman Etherington have recently described the resulting emergence of substantial African capitalist farmers in several areas of nineteenth-century South Africa: one or two thousand in the Cape alone in 1890, according to Bundy's estimate,[70] and smaller but unknown numbers in Natal[71] and elsewhere. The process began in the 1830s when the first Africans used ox-ploughs and it culminated in the 1870s and 1880s when the discovery of diamonds and gold expanded the market for agricultural products. Commissioners studying one such community in Thembuland in 1882 found individual African farmers who owned over 3000 acres of land, 200 cattle, 40 horses, or 500 small stock, plus ploughs and wagons.[72] As large employers of labour, these capitalist farmers held attitudes indistinguishable from those of their white counterparts. One who discussed 'the servant problem' with a commission of enquiry in the early 1890s explained that he avoided employing educated men: 'The educated man wants high wages; I endeavour to get the cheapest labour.' Another demanded stern penalties against squatters:

> We would like to have a severe law to deal with them. Because we are black you may perhaps think that we have sympathy with other black fellows who go to gaol, but as a fact we are just as great enemies of bad black people as white people are.[73]

Yet this brash and vigorous African capitalism was doomed. From the 1890s, and perhaps even earlier, white competition for land and markets and labour, backed by legislation imposed by growing white political power, destroyed South Africa's first black capitalism. By 1913 only a few wealthy

African farmers survived and the Land Act of that year, together with population growth in the Reserves, soon destroyed even those. Only very recently has African rural capitalism returned to South Africa.

From this survey of African capitalism in the nineteenth century there are perhaps four conclusions to carry forward into the colonial period as the themes of these lectures. The first is to stress once more the diversity of pre-colonial Africa: the range of different modes of production that existed; the variety of merchant groups in terms of their origins, social situations, and commercial activities; the contrast – not, of course, as sharp as has been presented here – between those regions which were in contact with the world economy, consequently possessing capitalistic sectors, and those which were not. Although work on the emergence of capitalism within individual African societies has scarcely begun, it is clear that the first signs of capitalist relations were normally in the spheres of trade, crafts, and urban life. In agriculture, production for exchange was common, but production by means of hired labour was rare except in the special case of South Africa. Yet what was perhaps most important for the future was the imbalance between developments in the agricultural and non-agricultural sectors. That has been a leading theme in the history of African capitalism to this day.

The second general point must be put in the form of a question: under what circumstances did capitalism take root most successfully in production, and why? Why was it in porterage, indigo-dyeing, and South African commercial farming that wage relationships seem to have developed most fully? One reason may have been that new labour relationships were profitable to the employer where an occupation either had no traditional labour organisation or was expanding too fast for the existing system to supply the necessary labour. The expansion of porterage in nineteenth-century East Africa, of commercial farming in South Africa, and of dyed cloth production in Kano would all suggest that. But a second point is that whether wage relationships emerged depended also on whether the previous labour force, if one existed, wished and was able to resist such an innovation. If Dr Shea is correct, Kano's skilled and strongly organised cloth-beaters were much more successful than its dyers in maintaining control over their occupation. One aspect of caste organisation was that it enabled a group to monopolise the advantages of an occupation and resist outside interference in it. The transition from one kind of labour relationship to another is generally a consequence of struggle, whose outcome is not always certain and may often result in some compromise and hybrid arrangement. That too we shall often find in the twentieth century.

Thirdly, the emergence of capitalism everywhere in nineteenth-century Africa was constrained by social systems. Patterns of marriage, inheritance, and family tradition were almost certainly among these constraints, although we know very little about the inheritance practices of African merchant groups. Related to these were the constraints imposed by the traditions of lineage, clientelist, and slave-owning societies which measured a man's prestige by the number of his kin or his dependants, requiring him to be ever dispersing his capital through investment in people. A visitor to the Yoruba of Nigeria in the 1860s reported, 'A man's position in society is estimated either by his bravery in war, or his wealth; and he can only manifest the latter by the number of his wives, children and slaves. From this circumstance men are frequently reported wealthy, and yet in emergencies can not raise ten bags of cowries (about $40).'[74] As an Agni proverb from Ivory Coast puts it, 'The rich man is like the pool where all the birds of the world come to drink.'[75] And in that formulation lies a larger issue which is much in need of thought and research. The ethos of African societies was pragmatic and this-worldly, with a strong element of hedonism: 'a religion of abundant life and the fullness of days', as Evans-Pritchard wrote of the Nuer, with a pragmatic willingness to adopt any device or innovation which might bring those benefits, and with a strong tendency to associate material prosperity with spiritual force.[76] Few African peoples had ascetic traditions. Admittedly there were exceptions. The national saint of Ethiopia, St Takla Haymanot, is believed to have stood praying on one leg for twenty-seven years until the other leg fell off and rose to heaven by itself. Islamic cenobites of Bornu in northern Nigeria were reported to 'dig a hole and make a tunnel and provision it with a little flour and water. This they enter after having repeated sayings taught them by their Shaykh, and stay there forty days and sometimes some of them die from hunger or thirst.'[77] Some of Africa's pastoralists – notably the Fulani of West Africa – had indigenous ascetic traditions of great interest, while certain long-established agricultural peoples like the Sénoufo of Ivory Coast cultivated an ethic of rustic humility and austerity.[78] Yet these were exceptions. Why asceticism was so rare in African cultures is itself an intriguing question – poverty is only a partial explanation – but the norm was certainly a frank enjoyment of pleasure amidst a life often harsh and insecure. This hedonistic pragmatism is to be seen moulded for ever in the rolls of fat around the necks of the bronze and terracotta heads from Ife. It was to be found in the ceremonial of great courts like that of Asante, where, so the first European visitor was told, the height of well-being was to run one's fingers through a fine beard wet with palm wine.[79] It was to be heard in the villages of Ibo country in eastern Nigeria, where a man who had gained the coveted Ozo title by displaying his wealth was accompanied through the streets by people chanting, 'Has money, Has money'.[80] It is to be found today expressed magnificently in the plays of Wole Soyinka:

> The world is not a constant honey-pot.
> Where I found little I made do with little.
> Where there was plenty I gorged myself.
> My master's hands and mine have always
> Dipped together and, home or sacred feast,
> The bowl was beaten bronze, the meats
> So succulent our teeth accused us of neglect.[81]

For us the central question is whether this hedonistic pragmatism was and is an obstacle to African capitalism, whether it encouraged acquisition but discouraged accumulation, whether it stood in the path of the 'worldly asceticism' which Weber said was the key to the distinctiveness of European capitalism.[82]

Finally, this survey of capitalism in pre-colonial Africa has shown the vital role of political action in its success or failure. White missionaries and officials gave black South African capitalist farmers the security they needed in order to succeed; white governments destroyed them when they succeeded too well. In Buganda, in Bulozi, in Asante the political order set its constraints on the emergence of capitalist relations. 'The king', an early ruler of Dahomey declared, 'shall inherit even the fly-swish of the leper.'[83] The role of the state has been crucial in the history of African capitalism, and that too is a theme which will lead us into the colonial period.

2 Capitalists and Peasants

In the nineteenth century the few elements of African capitalism that existed in sub-Saharan Africa were confined almost entirely to commerce, crafts, and the towns, except in the south. European conquest transformed this pattern. Admittedly, it is mistaken (although common) to think that African craft industries were everywhere destroyed by the competition of European manufactured goods, for many West African textile industries still flourish today.[1] And it is equally mistaken (and equally common) to think that African traders were everywhere driven out of business by European competition or changes in economic structure. Some were, especially those engaged in international trade. The extensive African commerce of the Senegal Valley was largely destroyed by French penetration, while Malam Yaroh of Zinder, once the leading African trader between modern Niger and North Africa, was reduced to scraping a living by selling charms.[2] But other African commercial groups survived to become nuclei of capitalism in the later colonial period. In Nigeria, for example, the African merchants of Lagos – that 'island of shopkeepers'[3] – prospered as the British established peace and better communications in the hinterland, while their northern counterparts in Kano benefited from the arrival of a railway and a new export crop, groundnuts.[4] Kano, moreover, had the advantage that the bulk of its commerce was regional rather than international, for it was generally those African traders engaged in internal commerce who best survived and even expanded under European rule[5] – a subject much in need of research.

Nevertheless, in the early colonial period the growth-points of African capitalism did generally move away from trade and industry into agriculture, just as they moved away from the West African savanna and the South African Cape to the high-rainfall areas of eastern and western Africa. This lecture will consider the growth of rural capitalism in tropical Africa during the last century, concentrating especially on how capitalist farming first took root in Africa's pre-capitalist rural societies and why, once rooted, it often struggled with such difficulty to survive.

A study of this subject must begin in Ghana, partly because Ghana's experience illustrates the two main issues most vividly and partly because it was in Ghana that the modern study of African rural capitalism began, in 1956, when Dr Polly Hill published her first book on the cocoa farmers of the southern Gold Coast.[6] She showed how, from the 1880s, the Akwapim and certain other peoples of the Accra hinterland migrated into neighbouring areas of virgin forest to purchase land and clear it for cocoa farms, sometimes even pledging their children in order to raise the money. Other Gold Coast peoples imitated them until by 1911 there may have been a thousand square miles of cocoa in the Gold Coast and it was the world's leading exporter.[7] Similar groups of innovators pioneered commercial farming in many other parts of the continent. In the most remote areas – the forests of western Ivory Coast, for example – the process is still going on, but the main expansion took place in the two periods during the last century when primary products commanded high prices on the world market, one running from the 1890s into the 1920s and the other occurring in the 1950s. The pioneers frequently carved out their farms on the frontiers of existing settlements where they obtained land most easily and met least resistance from the pre-capitalist order. The effort involved was often enormous. To clear one acre of virgin forest in West Africa may mean removing 500 tons of vegetation – 'not the sort of meat an old woman's teeth can chew', as a Ghanaian put it.[8] To understand African rural capitalism in its pioneer days one must see it as part of the larger history of the colonisation of the continent.

Moreover, to understand the pioneers one must know how they obtained the labour for their massive enterprise.[9] For the Akwapim and their fellows the answer is not entirely clear, but their sources of labour seem to have changed with time. The pioneers of the late nineteenth century hired porters to transport their cocoa, but to clear the forest and cultivate their farms they relied chiefly on family labour. After 1900, however, paid agricultural workers from less favoured regions became available for the first time and relationships moved closer towards a capitalist pattern.[10] The Akwapim in particular used *nkotokuano* workers – so called from the local word for bags or loads – who harvested cocoa in return for a fixed sum per load, while other large-scale cocoa planters employed contract workers either by the year or for specific tasks.[11] The first twenty or thirty years of the twentieth century were the heyday of pioneer capitalism, but by the 1930s the pattern of employment in the cocoa industry was moving away from wage relationships. Between 1932 and 1935 a British agricultural officer, W. H. Beckett, studied in great detail a cocoa-growing village named Akokoaso. He found that more than half the work on cocoa farms was done by the farmers and their families. Annual or casual workers did 10 per cent of the work. There were no nkotokuano workers. Instead, the remaining 34 per cent of labour was performed by a new category of workers called abusa-men.[12] *Abusa* means a one-third share and the practice of dividing returns into one-third shares was an old one in the southern Gold Coast. At Akokoaso abusa-men were caretakers who looked after other people's farms in return for a one-third share of the crop – sharecroppers, in fact, who used their own tools rather than those of their employers. Beckett found that they were hired chiefly by elderly farm-owners and only on farms already producing cocoa. Akokoaso, however, was a remote village whose small cocoa farms were owned by local people rather than migrant farmers. When Beckett moved on to study a large 'stranger' cocoa plantation in the late 1930s he found that almost all cocoa was still produced by nkotokuano workers, whose reward amounted to 16 per cent of the crop. But when he returned to the same farm in 1944 he found that the workers there had also come to receive a one-third share.[13]

By the 1930s, then, there was a trend towards abusa sharecropping on mature farms. The trend continued, for when Hill made her study of southern Gold Coast cocoa farming in the 1950s she found in some regions that three-quarters of the crop was picked by abusa sharecroppers.[14] For the employer, sharecropping was the least profitable form of labour,[15] although probably the easiest to supervise and finance. The workers, on the other hand, preferred sharecropping because it gave them control over their labour and enabled some to acquire cocoa farms of their own, for these men were 'at once entrepreneurs and workers'[16] and a number aspired to be agricultural colonists like their employers. The trend towards abusa relationships during the second quarter of this century was therefore a result of the growing age of cocoa farms and their owners, their shortage of working capital, and the workers' ability to advance their interests. A similar trend took place rather later in neighbouring Ivory Coast and is still going on there in the western frontier region.[17]

In 1957 Ghana became independent. Since then patterns of employment have shown much regional variation, but two points have been clear. First, in the 1970s most cocoa was still produced by sharecroppers, especially in the more recently developed cocoa areas.[18] Second, in the oldest cocoa regions even that pattern was often disintegrating. Again Akokoaso provides the model. In 1970 the village was resurveyed, rather hastily. It now had fewer abusa caretakers than in the 1930s. Those who remained looked after larger acreages, less carefully, for half rather than one-third of the crop, and had often succeeded in establishing their own cocoa farms as well. By contrast, the most common kind of worker in Akokoaso in 1970 appeared to be the casual labourer, who in the 1930s had supplied only 8 per cent of labour needs.[19] The reason for this was that Akokoaso had been impoverished by cocoa tree diseases, ageing trees, and declining real producer prices. Yields were too poor to attract sharecroppers and farmers were too poor to pay for anything but occasional casual labour. Output figures showed the result. Ghana's cocoa production has seen two peaks, one in the mid-1930s (following high prices and extensive plantings in the 1920s) and the other in the mid-1960s (following high prices in the 1950s). Since the mid-1960s, however, output has declined rapidly. In 1981 the marketed crop was only half that of the mid-1960s[20] and one perceptive observer asked whether Ghana was to become another of those areas like the West Indies or the Scottish Highlands which had been abandoned once the world economy no longer needed their speciality.[21] In March 1982, on the twenty-fifth anniversary of Ghana's independence, Flight-Lieutenant Rawlings said that his regime's first economic priority was the rehabilitation of traditional foreign exchange earnings, meaning the cocoa industry.[22]

This account of labour relationships in Ghanaian cocoa-farming will introduce the first of the two questions to be asked about capitalist farming: how it first took root in Africa's pre-capitalist rural societies. As we have seen, nineteenth-century rural Africa supported several pre-capitalist modes of production: domestic or lineage production, clientage or tributary relations, slavery, and various combinations of these. The question is whether the rural capitalism that emerged in different areas varied according to the different pre-capitalist modes of production in those areas, and varied in some regular way. I am anxious to pose this very difficult question, although I have only tentative answers to suggest.

Clearly, the evolution of capitalist agriculture among the Akwapim was shaped by their previous economic experience, chiefly in two ways. First, it was several centuries of foreign trade, and especially the recent export of palm produce and rubber, that gave Akwapim the initial capital to buy land and hire porters, while the porters themselves, as we have seen, were the one category of paid workers existing outside the towns in the southern Gold Coast at this time. In other words, Akwapim rural capitalism was from the beginning shaped by the fact that a capitalistic sector of exchange already existed in the Gold Coast, and by the character of that sector. This was to be a common pattern throughout sub-Saharan Africa: where a capitalistic sector existed, it provided the channel through which the stimuli to capitalist production penetrated. Thus, probably the first large-scale black employers of more or less free labour in West Africa were the Afro-American settlers in Liberia who first established themselves as merchants and then in the 1840s and 1850s began to create sugar and coffee plantations in a country where formal slavery was outlawed from the beginning.[23] They were followed from 1880 by the African traders of Lagos, who established plantations on the nearby mainland; one of these, J. K. Coker, regularly employed some 200 migrant workers at the turn of the century, treating them in a paternalistic manner and teaching them about new crops, literacy, and his own version of independent Christianity.[24] Another very early West African plantation owner was the lawyer Sir Samuel Lewis of Freetown in Sierra Leone, the first African to receive a knighthood; it is recorded that eighty of his labourers marched behind the family hammocks to church on Sunday mornings.[25]

The second way in which Akwapim capitalism was shaped by previous economic experience was that the early cocoa planters could not draw on a subordinate labour force of cultivators from within their own society, because it lacked either strong political authorities or marked class distinctions. Instead, as we have seen, they had to rely first on family labour and then on long-distance migrants whose bargaining power bred the abusa sharecropping system, itself an adaptation of traditional practices. In this, Akwapim experience contrasted with the growth of capitalist cocoa farming in Asante, slightly to the northwest, where both slavery and clientage existed and many early cocoa farmers were chiefs and rich merchants who controlled both capital in the form of gold and labour in the form of slaves.[26] Although northern labourers were migrating to Asante to 'sell their hoes', as they put it, by the First World War,[27] nevertheless Gareth Austin's study of cocoa growing in southern Asante has shown that pre-capitalist relations of production predominated there until the 1920s: kinship, slavery, pawnship, clientage, and political subjection.[28] Until his work is published, however, we do not know how the subsequent transition to capitalist relationships took place in Asante. To examine that in areas with different pre-capitalist modes of production it is best to turn to East Africa.

The kingdom of Buganda offers unusually detailed evidence of the process by which pre-capitalist relations of production – clientage, slavery, and lineage ties – were transformed into capitalist relations. The first attempts by missionaries to employ hired workers in the 1880s were resisted by Buganda's rulers. The next attempts were resisted by Buganda's workers. In 1894 an unusually perceptive missionary, Robert Walker, reported that he had offered to pay men living on mission land to perform a task over and above their normal obligation to supply tributary labour. The response took him aback:

> They refused most indignantly and said did I suppose they would accept pay from their masters. So we arranged it in this way, as a kindness they would build the house, and I promised them some [cowrie] shells to buy a bit of beef with when the job is finished. To this they agreed if it was quite understood that they were not paid for their work. They seemed to think that to be paid would be as bad as stealing on their part.[29]

In the same year, however, Buganda became a British Protectorate and change accelerated. In 1895 Walker described the Chief Minister of Buganda, Apolo Kaggwa, paying his own followers for their work, probably for the first time. The men were building Kaggwa a two-storey house of sun-dried brick. 'So great is the dislike to handling the clay', Walker reported, 'that he has to pay one [cowrie] shell a brick to his own men'[30] – scarcely capitalism, perhaps, but the process is important: it was generally in novel occupations that wage relations were first superimposed on pre-capitalist patterns, often at the workers' insistence.[31] Kaggwa's example spread fast. Only three years later Walker recorded an African clergyman denouncing from the pulpit the fact that 'no one would work without being paid for it. That whereas formerly boys and girls went off to the woods to bring firewood for their masters as a matter of course, now they all required paying for it.'[32] Another two years and Walker was bewailing the end of the old Buganda:

> The chiefs are all anxious to be traders, and it is with some feelings of regret that I see a shop has been built just inside the royal gateway. Where armed men stood in barbaric splendour when I first came to the country [twelve years earlier], you see now a shop with cheap calicoes for sale, a fragment of Petticoat Lane, but with more fun about it, as the lads who act as shopmen often try the clothes on.[33]

That was in 1900. In the same year Walker himself helped to negotiate an agreement between the British and the Baganda leaders which created an entirely new system of private landownership in Buganda, converting chiefs into landowners and their followers into tenants. Some of the new landowners set themselves up as capitalist farmers. In 1912 some were said to have 'large rubber and coffee plantations' and were becoming very rich men.[34] Commonly these farmers either used their tenants' tributary labour or allowed them to commute it into cash and then used the money to pay hired workers, so that pre-capitalist relations provided the shade beneath which capitalism took root. Most landowners preferred to draw rent from their tenants rather than farming the land themselves, but they too relied on pre-capitalist ties. In the Luganda language the word meaning 'to rent land', *okusenga*, is the same word that in the pre-capitalist order had meant 'to join a chief's service', and that in turn was related to the word meaning to form a line of battle.[35] These were only some of the many ways in which early twentieth-century Baganda absorbed capitalist relations into their still predominantly pre-capitalist society.

On the surface it might seem that such continuities between capitalist and pre-capitalist relations of production would have been stronger in class societies than among those practising a domestic mode of production, but in fact it has been the domestic mode where continuities have been traced most assiduously. In East Africa the outstanding work is Michael Cowen's study of the northern Kikuyu of the Nyeri district in Kenya. There most of the first African capitalist farmers who emerged in the 1920s were sons of wealthy stockowners of the pre-colonial period. But they were characteristically those sons who had been to mission schools and obtained skilled or semi-skilled jobs which gave them the capital to employ labour and also obliged them to do so, since they were often absent and, as young monogamous Christians, lacked family members to work for them.[36]

This tendency for the modern-sector employee to become the rural employer is described by Cowen as 'straddling' and has become a key concept in the analysis of African capitalism in eastern and southern Africa. It has been observed (with variations) in Uganda,[37] Zaire,[38] Zambia,[39] and Zimbabwe,[40] while Gavin Kitching has made it the core of his analysis of differentiation in colonial Kenya, a country where the domestic mode of production was especially predominant before European conquest. Kitching has stressed in particular that commodity production by absentee males threw much of the labour on to women, so that bridewealth was commercialised and increased while the status of women declined.[41] One important comparative question about African capitalism is whether the 'straddling' process was equally widespread throughout the continent. 'Scholar-farmers', as Dr Hill calls them,[42] were certainly very common in West Africa – extensively among Liberian rubber-planters, for example[43] – but, despite this, 'straddling' was probably less important in areas where other opportunities to accumulate capital were available, whether through the existence of pre-colonial capitalistic sectors, as in many parts of West Africa, or through the exploitation of pre-capitalist inequalities, as in Buganda.

In East Africa, then, there are examples of capitalist relations emerging in the early colonial period in pre-capitalist class societies like Buganda and in lineage societies like the

Kikuyu. Students of African capitalism have often argued that certain pre-capitalist modes of production were more fertile soil than others for the development of capitalism. In Ivory Coast, for example, Samir Amin claimed that capitalist relations developed more rapidly among stratified Akan-speaking groups than among stateless peoples, because prior stratification enabled aristocrats to control land and exploit labour.[44] By contrast, another authority, Pierre-Philippe Rey, has argued exactly the opposite: that capitalism developed most easily in Africa's lineage societies.[45] In reality, as the East African evidence shows, capitalism – once stimulated from outside – could evolve equally well in any pre-capitalist mode of production; the interesting question is whether it evolved in different ways, and one major difference was probably the varying importance of the straddling process. But it is clear that in all the cases we have examined, capitalist relations initially utilised those non-economic means of exploiting labour which existed in pre-capitalist societies, whether they were the Muganda commoner's allegiance to his chief or the Kikuyu wife's subordination to her husband.

These issues have been conceptualised by Marxists as 'the articulation of modes of production'. They argue that any concrete social formation, except perhaps the hunting band, contains more than one mode of production, or elements of more than one. Articulation is the interrelation between them. The most penetrating theorist, Pierre-Philippe Rey, takes as his model the evolution of capitalism within European feudalism.[46] He claims that this was made possible only by conditions resulting from the development of the feudal system: a body of landless wage-labourers, a marketable food surplus, and non-self-sufficient consumers to absorb the products of capitalist manufacture. Thus Rey argues that capitalism grew up under the protection of feudalism, whose legacies (notably ground rent) survived into it, and he claims that capitalism took root in other pre-capitalist modes through similar processes. The initial relationship between them was exchange, from which the dominant pre-capitalist groups benefited. To secure goods from the capitalist sector, they supplied it with labour mobilised through the non-economic means of exploitation existing in the pre-capitalist society, such as the control of marriageable women by older men which obliged younger men to work in order to accumulate bridewealth. Eventually the pre-capitalist economy might be so undermined that sheer economic need forced workers into the capitalist sector, first as temporary migrants, then as permanent proletarians, until finally capitalist relations might permeate the society. The key role in the whole process was that of the dominant groups in the pre-capitalist order: the landowning chiefs in Buganda, the wealthy cattle-owners in Nyeri.

Its most acid critic has observed that 'articulation . . . a term deriving from anatomy, a science whose demonstration requires that the subject be dead',[47] and there are many who would like an invitation to the funeral. I still hope for recovery, however, because I see the concept as potentially a valuable way of generalising about the enormous variety of circumstances and consequences attending the emergence of capitalism in different parts of Africa. But to accommodate that diversity, the theory must be made more flexible. Two suggestions might be made. One problem is that Rey constructed his model from the single case of Congo-Brazzaville where he did his fieldwork. This led him to assume that much violence necessarily accompanied the penetration of capitalism, that the capitalist sector of the economy would inevitably be controlled by Europeans, and that Africans would enter it as migrant labourers, thus enabling the elders to remain dominant by siphoning off the young men's earnings. In reality, however, there were many areas in early colonial Africa where articulation operated not through the dominant groups of the pre-capitalist order but through the dominated. In Yorubaland and among the Beti and their neighbours in southern Cameroun, for example, young men left home to take up employment or trade in the capitalist sector as a positive liberation from control by their elders.[48] For another group in southern Cameroun, the Maka, it has been shown that articulation was the work of young men who entered the capitalist economy not as migrant labourers but as cash-crop growers,[49] a pattern often found both among Gold Coast cocoa growers and elsewhere in the continent.

The second difficulty with the notion of articulation is whether the process is thought to be self-sustaining. Rey originally argued that capitalism, once rooted in a pre-capitalist economy, would expand to supplant it, much as Marx claimed in 1853. Later, however, Rey suggested instead that capitalism might rather preserve, fossilise, and exploit pre-capitalist modes, as has been the predominant view among dependency theorists.[50] Both views seem unduly rigid and it is worth noting that Marx envisaged three rather than two alternatives. 'In all conquests', he wrote, 'there are three possibilities. The conquering nation subjects the conquered nation to its own mode of production . . .; or it allows the old mode to remain and is content with tribute . . . ; or interaction takes place, which gives rise to a new system, a synthesis.'[51] These have indeed been the three alternative paths available to African capitalism once it was rooted in a particular society. The paths have not been entirely distinct, for an element of synthesis has been present in every case. But the interesting question is why capitalism has sustained its momentum and steadily dissolved older social orders in some areas of Africa; why it has failed to sustain that momentum and instead has become merely parasitic on the old order in other areas; and why complex syntheses of capitalist and pre-capitalist relations have come into being elsewhere. That is the subject of the remainder of this lecture.

Once more the starting-point is the impasse which capitalism reached in the Ghanaian cocoa industry.[52] The growth of sharecropping in place of wage relations resulted from the ageing of the cocoa trees and their owners, from shortage of working capital, from the difficulty of directly managing capitalist enterprises, and from the bargaining power of workers anxious to control their own time and possibly to establish their own plantations. The more recent abandonment even of sharecropping in certain areas was due to the continued decay of old cocoa trees, the depredations of disease, the inability of cocoa farmers to maintain their momentum of accumulation in face of the extraction of surplus by a marketing system dominated first by expatriate trading companies and then by the state, and above all the ruthless exploitation of Ghana's cocoa industry in the name of 'development' by the departing colonial government and its African successors. Thus, apart from the special local circumstances of disease and ageing, the impasse of Ghanaian rural capitalism resulted from three forces: the continuing resistance of pre-capitalist elements (as in the sharecroppers' struggle to avoid proletarianisation), the constraints imposed by the world economy, and the actions of the state.

These three forces appeared repeatedly in other areas of Africa where rural capitalism failed to supplant pre-capitalist relations. The important point is to see all three forces acting together, rather than stressing one or another as much recent work has done. Of the resources which pre-capitalist groups could set against the growth of capitalism, the most important was Africa's abundant land, not so much because this inhibited the emergence of freehold property – for capitalism can flourish under many land tenure systems short of freehold – but because it enabled most rural peoples to preserve their household economies and ensured that wage-earners generally had to be drawn as temporary migrants from remote areas. That workers were migrants did not itself prevent employers from being capitalists (or we should be describing the Anglo-American Corporation as a pre-capitalist institution), nor did it inhibit capitalist relationships at the point of production (although it probably strengthened the workers in the class struggle which always determines the intensity of work[53]), but migrant labour did check the formation of capitalist and proletarian classes. Moreover, African societies had other means of resisting capitalism. The sheer hostility and unpredictability of their environment, as Dr Hill has shown for

Hausaland, was itself a major obstacle to the emergence of self-reproducing classes of rural capitalists. Partible inheritance and especially polygyny were important social obstacles to class formation; in southern Cameroun and northern Gabon these have probably been major reasons why cocoa growing has developed as a peasant rather than a capitalist enterprise.[54] By these and other means many African societies maintained resistance to capitalist penetration over very long periods. In a recent study of the lower Zambesi Valley in Mozambique, where huge Portuguese estates existed from the seventeenth century until the 1970s, the authors have shown that the 'peasant alternative' survived throughout the period, reappearing whenever the estate-owners weakened and economic circumstances favoured small producers.[55] Even more striking, perhaps, has been the modern history of Zanzibar, where peasants have successfully resisted domination first by Arab slave-owners, then by aspiring Arab capitalists backed by the British authorities, and finally by aspiring African socialists following the revolution of 1964.[56] All Africa's genuine revolutions have resulted in the reconquest of the land by the peasantry – a subject considered again in the next lecture.

The second major obstacle to the growth of rural capitalism lay in the constraints imposed by the international economy. Twice, in the 1930s and 1960s, the collapse of world commodity prices helped to frustrate emerging capitalist classes. Moreover, international capital has repeatedly sought to prevent the emergence of rural capitalists in Africa, preferring instead to deal directly with small peasant producers whose bargaining power was weaker. In the Gold Coast, for example, the cocoa-buying firms combined in the 1930s to undermine the African cocoa brokers who were the most prominent indigenous capitalists.[57] In the Sudan it has been argued persuasively that the Gezira irrigation scheme, where peasants grew cotton as tenants first of a metropolitan company and then of the Sudanese government, has tended to obstruct the emergence of large producers with their own capital, certainly when compared with their appearance in the neighbouring rain-fed grainlands.[58] There is much truth in the notion that the concern to benefit the peasant producer which contemporary aid donors show in certain (but by no means all) African countries is calculated to prevent the emergence of indigenous capitalist classes.

In this respect the aid donors are heirs to colonial governments, who were themselves heirs to Africa's pre-colonial rulers. Except in Southern Rhodesia, European governments were uniformly hostile to African rural capitalism, seeing it not only as socially and politically dangerous but as somehow improper for Africans, like guitars or three-piece suits. In 1924 an otherwise sympathetic district officer wrote from Kilimanjaro in Tanganyika:

The aim has been to promote coffee growing as a peasant cultivation, each one working his plot by his own industry with the help of his women and children, so that a class of native employers is not evolved, or at any rate is restricted to a small number comprising only prominent persons. A plantation of 500 trees may with careful attention to their cultivation give from 250 s. up to 500 s. p.a. which is as much as the ordinary native can make proper use of.[59]

A few years later the Tanganyika government deliberately destroyed the emerging African farmer-traders of the coffee-growing areas and replaced them with state-controlled co-operative societies.[60] In the Gold Coast, similarly, government moved against the African cocoa brokers in 1939, and thereafter the official marketing boards established throughout British Africa expropriated much of the surplus which might have fuelled rural capitalism. Only in the 1950s did African capitalists suddenly become attractive to Europeans who were desperately seeking like-minded black successors, and then the successors often proved only too like-minded, for many African governments, as we shall see, have been equally hostile to the growth of rural capitalism. It has been estimated that the producer price of cocoa in Cameroun in 1976 was roughly 10 per cent of the world price.[61]

In all these ways, then, the momentum of rural capitalism was checked. But it was not usually checked completely. The most common outcome of articulation in twentieth-century Africa has been what Marx called an 'interaction' with the old mode of production 'which gives rise to a new system, a synthesis'. To see the creation of such a synthesis, it is best to return to Buganda. Up to the First World War capitalism was certainly developing rapidly there, although it was still contained within a predominantly pre-capitalist society. Thereafter, however, the further growth of capitalist relations met a series of checks. In the 1920s peasant protest led the sympathetic British authorities to fix at low levels the rent and labour tribute which landowners might exact from their tenants. This encouraged landowners to sell parcels of land to peasants, so that whereas the implementation of the agreement of 1900 had divided the land of Buganda among some 4000 owners, by the mid-1960s the number of Baganda owning freehold land had risen to about 112,000. Moreover, after the First World War an influx of impoverished migrant labourers from outside Buganda enabled even the peasant cotton grower to employ seasonal labour, thereby inhibiting class formation among Baganda.[62]

In the early 1930s Professor Lucy Mair worked in the Buganda countryside and described a society which was an intricate and fascinating blend of pre-capitalist and capitalist relations. 'Every one who can afford it now pays labourers from other tribes to do such rough work as clearing fresh ground', she reported, but 'the relationship between the family and the labourers is generally a very amicable one. When there is a visitor, the hired man comes and sits in the doorway and listens to the conversation.'[63] Even landlords who held no official positions were treated as chiefs, the rent-restriction law bound the tenant to render his landlord 'all respect and obedience prescribed by native law and custom',[64] and the advent of freehold land had positively strengthened family ties by providing for the first time something that was worth inheriting.[65] On a wall Professor Mair saw the proverb: 'A shilling in the house is worth a thousand at the bank.'[66] It was an apt summary of Buganda's novel synthesis of pre-capitalist and capitalist values. A generation later, in the 1950s, a new group of large farmers emerged, this time growing coffee and coming mainly from peasant families, but as rural capitalists they too were unconvincing, for most were elderly men, often virtually retired to the countryside, who had few plans for further innovation, were educating their sons for careers outside agriculture, intended to divide their farms among their heirs, and generally farmed on a large scale only during that part of their life cycle when they had many children to support.[67] It seems unlikely that they could have established a self-reproducing rural capitalism, but we shall never know, for little of their activity can have survived the chaos of the last two decades.

Such syntheses of capitalist and pre-capitalist elements have been the normal pattern of Africa's more prosperous rural societies during this century. Precisely such a synthesis was described, for example, in the most detailed study of a cash-crop economy ever made in Africa: the survey of Yoruba cocoa farmers made in 1951–2 by Galletti and his colleagues.[68] The most interesting question, however, is whether rural capitalism has anywhere advanced beyond such a synthesis to become predominant and self-reproducing. The test case is certainly Kenya.

Here again the basic work has been Dr Cowen's. Having shown the emergence of Kikuyu rural entrepreneurs from the stock-owning families, the mission schools, and the straddling process during the 1920s, Cowen has also shown that their hopes of further accumulation from the production of wattle were checked in the 1930s by the intervention of international capital and the state. With government support, the world's largest wattle-producing company generalised the crop among the Kikuyu and fixed maximum acreages, thus depriving aspiring capitalists of both their labour force and their economies of scale. The Mau Mau rebellion of 1952 was, in Dr Cowen's analysis, mainly an attempt by frustrated bourgeois forces to free themselves from constraint by the colonial order. Its defeat was followed by a further setback for rural capitalism when pioneer Kikuyu dairy farmers and cash-crop growers were undercut by the British government's land consolidation and agricultural improvement programme, which enabled all but the weakest peasant households to resist proletarianisation. Since Kenya's independence, the alliance between international capital, the aid agencies, and the middle peasantry has enabled petty commodity production to maintain its resistance to rural capitalism.[69]

This is a powerful argument and has had great influence on recent thinking about African capitalism. But it has been equally strongly contested, especially in the work of Dr Apollo Njonjo.[70] While accepting the emergence of the rural entrepreneurs and their frustration between the wars, Njonjo sees Mau Mau as essentially an anti-capitalist rebellion by dispossessed Kikuyu, 'a violent attempt to stop the capitalist transition'.[71] Its defeat therefore opened the way to the triumph of capitalism in Kenya, sweeping away the outdated racial constraints of the colonial period and creating a social order based on an implicit alliance between African capitalists and the middle peasantry, an alliance sealed by their common interest in freehold ownership of land, in extending commodity production, and in dominating and exploiting the landless, of whom there were probably nearly half a million by the late 1970s.[72] Meanwhile, so other scholars have argued, the 1970s witnessed further advance by African capitalists into manufacturing industry, urban property, and the most modern plantation agriculture – between 1973 and 1977 Africans bought 57 per cent of Kenya's foreign-owned coffee estates.[73] At the same time the land consolidation programme was extending nascent capitalism away from the Kikuyu heartland into the other regions of Kenya. A study of the Mbeere people in the lowlands to the southeast of Mount Kenya in 1977 showed that the largest 25 per cent of farms occupied 58 per cent of the land in one location. Land consolidation had sharply reduced the level of social interaction in Mbeere. People went to extraordinary lengths to avoid eating or drinking at each other's homes. Communal labour groups had given way to hired labour. Fences and 'Keep Out!' notices had blossomed. 'Today, in many parts of Mbeere, every plant has an owner who restricts its use by others', investigators reported. 'And a small but increasing number of people have rights to neither land nor plants.' Secondary school students familiar with the works of Chinua Achebe compared Mbeere in 1977 to *Things Fall Apart*.[74]

It is impossible here to resolve this very important conflict of views on Kenyan capitalism. I suspect that the truth lies between the two arguments and that the real situation has been more complicated than either suggests. The Mau Mau rebellion, for example, was a composite movement embracing the grievances both of many frustrated entrepreneurs and of the dispossessed. Its defeat did lead to the triumph of private property and the class alliance which Dr Njonjo suggests, but the inherent antagonism between the two elements in the alliance – peasants and capitalists – has as yet scarcely begun to work itself out in struggle. Kenya is now clearly becoming a capitalist society – there will be more to say of this in the last lecture – but it is not clear whether the agricultural sector of that society will be dominated by large capitalist farms, small peasant holdings, or – an alternative as yet scarcely considered, but the one which accompanied the capitalist industrialisation of Japan – a pattern of capitalist landlords and peasant tenants. In recent years there have been trends in different directions: government has resisted populist demands for a ceiling on individual landholdings; Africans have bought an ever larger share of the country's modern farms; roughly one-third of the land which Africans acquired as large farms at independence has been subdivided into more efficient smallholdings; and yet even small-farm agriculture has become increasingly reliant on hired labour and is probably increasingly motivated by capitalist aspirations.[75] The future pattern of Kenyan agriculture is still entirely undecided. What is certain is that rural capitalism has already advanced further in Kenya than in any other country we have yet examined. One reason is that in the colonial period Kenya's European and Indian communities created a sector of modern capitalism which Africans have inherited. Another is that Kenya is unusually short of arable land, so that consolidation has been possible and has transformed property relationships. And the third is that the circumstances of Mau Mau and decolonisation established a regime with strong capitalist sympathies and formidable political skill. The role of the state, as ever, has been crucial to the development of Kenyan capitalism.

In Kenya, then, rural capitalism still has the possibility of destroying pre-capitalist relations of production. If we ask whether that possibility exists elsewhere in sub-Saharan Africa, three areas deserve consideration. One is Nigeria, where the massive agro-business schemes and other innovations of the last two decades have for the first time pushed rural capitalism beyond the synthesis with pre-capitalist relations which Hill found in Hausaland and Galletti and his colleagues observed among the Yoruba. But I shall have much to say in later lectures about Nigeria and also about a second country where a more advanced rural capitalism may have come into being, Ivory Coast. This lecture must end with a third region, southern Africa.

Perhaps the African country where the articulation of pre-capitalist and capitalist modes of production has taken place most smoothly is Botswana. Pre-colonial Tswana aristocrats enjoyed the labour of semi-servile dependants and owned the vast majority of cattle. When Khama became chief of the Bamangwato group among them in 1875, after they had been trading with the Cape for thirty years, he renounced royal claims over those cattle which were in the hands of aristocrats, thereby making it easier for them to accumulate independent wealth.[76] During the colonial period Tswana aristocrats not only took the lead in plough-farming and other modern innovations but also gained control of the campaign for political independence and the autonomous government which it produced. Botswana's first president was Sir Seretse Khama; its second, President Masire, is a wealthy cattle-owner and was the first Tswana to gain a Master Farmer's certificate from the British colonial authorities. Inequality of wealth has grown markedly in Botswana since independence and much land has been enclosed to the profit of wealthy cattle-owners.[77] Rural capitalism has also advanced in Swaziland and among the large African maize-growers of southern Zambia.[78]

But the most interesting place to watch will be Zimbabwe. On the one hand Zimbabwe has many of the same circumstances that have made Kenyan capitalism so vigorous. Zimbabwe has strong capitalist institutions created by a local white bourgeoisie, many of whom are now anxious to find black allies – the white and black Chambers of Commerce confederated in 1978. Zimbabwe has an aspiring black bourgeoisie eager to take over existing institutions, for capitalist farming has been encouraged since the 1930s in the Native Purchase Areas and in 1975 there were about a thousand African farmers owning an average of over a thousand acres each.[79] Zimbabwe, moreover, is subject to even stronger international pressures towards capitalism than were exerted on Kenya. But unlike Kenya, Zimbabwe has an African government which, at an ideological level, is seriously dedicated to socialist policies. There have already been reports of conflict between government and Africans buying former white farms privately.[80] The future of Zimbabwe will be a fascinating test of the relative strength in modern Africa of state policy as against inherited objective reality. And the future of Zimbabwe is absolutely vital to the future of capitalism in Africa.

3 Capitalists and Preachers

One day during 1848 the missionary Hope Masterton Waddell was invited to preach to the leading men of Old Calabar, a port in eastern Nigeria famous for its palm oil. Waddell was a man from the heart of Roger Anstey's world. Before settling in Old Calabar in 1846, he had worked for seventeen years as a Presbyterian missionary in Jamaica at the time when missionaries were seeking to teach the newly emancipated slaves the virtues of Victorian capitalism. Now, in his new post, Waddell seized the opportunity to preach the same gospel of Christianity and Commerce to the men of Old Calabar:

> I preached the way of wealth from the word of God, industry, honesty, economy, temperance, knowledge, and the blessing of God; warning against idleness, sloth, gluttony, drunkenness, ignorance, waste, and bad company, as the sure way to poverty and ruin. Seeing the company did not look pleased, I asked the king what ailed them. He said, that they knew all that themselves already.[1]

Old Calabar, of course, was exceptional. It had at least two centuries' experience of trade with Europeans and some of its leading men were accustomed to keep written records – even, in one surviving case, a diary – and to send their sons to school in England.[2] But the faith in hard work and self-advancement which its merchants shared with their would-be reformer was much more widely spread in pre-colonial Africa. One hundred miles to the west, in New Calabar, it has been suggested that

44

the competitive pursuit of status was as basic to the personalities of the people as sex was to Freud's Viennese.[3] And deep in the interior of Africa, among the Kuba people of southern Zaire, Professor Vansina tells us that in the late nineteenth century 'most Kuba worked from six in the morning to eight at night. A work ethic definitely existed. Kuba mythology as taught to boys in initiation equated laziness with the supreme evil: witchcraft.'[4] Such values were very widespread among Africa's agricultural peoples.

The point is central to the argument of this lecture. Waddell and the abolitionists in general believed that they must convert Africans to capitalist values, but in fact many of the values they sought to inculcate were already widely shared by Africans. What then, precisely, were the intellectual and ethical changes which Africans did have to make if they wished to become capitalists and employers of labour? What precisely could Christianity, or Islam, or Africa's indigenous religions contribute to a transition to capitalism? And what spiritual and cultural resources could Africans draw upon if they wanted to resist such a transition? These surely are questions that would have quickened Roger Anstey's pulse.

To answer them, the best place to begin is Zambia. There, in 1963, among the Lala people, Norman Long studied the recently emerged shopkeepers and progressive farmers who were known locally as the *bawina*, from the English word 'to win'.[5] He found that a disproportionately large number of them were also Jehovah's Witnesses and he set out to trace the connections between membership of that sect and commercial success. It was not, he found, that the sect greatly favoured capitalism. Indeed, it proclaimed that in the New Kingdom which was so soon to come, 'No-one will be working for another man.' Rather, membership encouraged commercial success in three less direct ways. First, certain of the Witnesses' specific teachings aided a businessman: the importance of literacy (in order to read the scriptures), the careful use of time, the notion that to acquire skills was to have them ready for the New Kingdom. Second, to be a Witness was to belong to a solidary community whose mutual trust gave its members an entrepreneurial advantage. And finally, since the Lala were a matrilineal people but the teachings of the Witnesses favoured patriliny, to become a Witness provided an ideological justification for cutting unwanted ties with matrilineal kin, who might otherwise eat up the profits of the enterprise, and for replacing their often inefficient assistance with hired labourers paid in cash. Among the Lala, then, it was not simply that Jehovah's Witnesses became capitalists, but that aspiring capitalists became Witnesses.

Such specific, identifiable links between Christianity and capitalism have been common in Africa. The traders of Lagos who established plantations on the mainland in the late nineteenth century, for example, were mostly zealous members of independent churches and created a symbiotic relationship between their churches and their plantations. Migrant labourers working on the plantations were taught independent Christianity. On returning home they sometimes founded daughter congregations and invited their employer-pastor to visit them. On the way he recruited new labourers for his plantation, and so the process continued.[6]

Christianity, then, could facilitate entrance into the role of capitalist. Could it also facilitate entrance into the role of worker, of anonymous member in large-scale capitalist society? This has recently been the subject of fascinating research in Ivory Coast by scholars, mostly French, working at the Christian healing centre at Bregbo, twenty miles east of Abidjan.[7] Bregbo is the creation of Albert Atcho, who was born there in 1903. After several years as a soldier, a chief, and an entrepreneur, he began his main career as a healer at Bregbo in 1948, working in the tradition of the Liberian prophet, William Wade Harris, who conducted a great evangelistic campaign in southern Ivory Coast in 1913 and 1914. What took people to Bregbo was sickness, physical or psychological. After a preliminary diagnosis, Atcho either prescribed a herbal remedy, directed the patient to a western-style hospital, sought divine guidance by telegram or telephone, or required the patient to make a confession on the grounds that his malady was a divine punishment for sin – and to go on confessing until he was cured. Each confession was recorded by a clerk in a school exercise book. By the early 1970s there were over 3000 texts for the French researchers to study.

Working so close to Abidjan, at the heart of the 'Ivoirian miracle', Atcho's ministry related to the growth of capitalism at many points. Himself a modernist and an entrepreneur, he preached a version of Christianity which scarcely mentioned the afterlife but grew directly out of the this-worldly hedonism of African religious tradition:

> What is the happiness that you desire to have? First, children, to be well paid in your job, to find a place of employment rapidly, to succeed in planting, and to have a better life.[8]

The model of prosperity was the European:

> If it were possible to see God, if there were someone whom one could see, it would not be a black man whom one would see but a white. Being white Himself, He created like Him the one who directly resembled Him. He confided to him all the notions, all the facilities and the technical abilities. That is why the whites are in advance of us. But in drawing nearer to God again our-selves, we shall become like our elder brothers the white men.[9]

In particular, Europeans knew how to make positive use of magic, whereas Africans used it only negatively to hold back those seeking to advance themselves.

At Bregbo a second and more profound interaction with capitalism appeared in the confessions made by patients. They revealed the tensions bred by employment relationships, for those who confessed that they belonged to covens of malefactors often listed migrant labourers as fellow members.[10] They revealed the desire for modern possessions: 'I had a telephone, as a devil'; 'I had a car, as a devil'.[11] More important, the confessions showed that many maladies were due to tensions between old kinship ties and the individualism demanded by the new Ivoirian society. As András Zempléni writes, Bregbo was concerned with 'one of the major problems of contemporary Africa: the process of individualisation'.[12] Atcho healed individuals; he did not stress the restoration of harmony to groups. He taught his patients not to believe that they suffered misfortune because they had been bewitched – the persecutive notion normal in small-scale agricultural societies. But he did not teach them to ascribe their misfortunes to their own guilt and thereby to internalise it and achieve individual, personal responsibility. Rather, he offered an escape from the full strains of individualisation by assuring his patients that their maladies were divine punishments for collaborating with the actions of the devil, and it was these actions that were vividly described in the thousands of imaginary confessions. In that it is the function of prophetism to ease historical transitions, Atcho was the prophet of Ivory Coast's transition to capitalism. And it was entirely in keeping with the association of spiritual force with material prosperity that he should have been not an ascetic but a wealthy entrepreneur. Africa is one continent where prophets do have honour in their own country.

Connections of this kind between Christianity and capitalism are familiar enough within European history[13] and I need not illustrate them further. But not all of Africa is Christian. Much of it is Muslim. Has Islam interacted with emerging capitalism in similar ways?

There is an almost exact parallel to the Jehovah's Witnesses of Zambia in David Parkin's study of adherence to Islam among the Giriama of the Kenyan coast.[14] A stateless people, the Giriama began to produce copra for the world market in the 1930s. Enterprising younger family heads began to accumulate land and coconut palms at the expense of the less far-sighted. In order to do so they did not resort to overtly capitalist methods, which would not have been socially acceptable, but forced their elders into debt or sale by means of competitive ostentation at weddings and funerals – a splendid example both of the exploitation of hedonistic values and of the way in which the articulation of capitalist and domestic modes of production might benefit the young rather than the old. By the 1960s the accumulators, as Parkin calls these enterprising younger men, commonly hired labour and had their land ploughed with tractors. Moreover, although the Giriama had long resisted the Islam of the East African coast, by the 1960s a number of the accumulators had become Muslims, usually as a result of possession by an 'Islamic spirit' and at least to the extent of observing Ramadan and eschewing alcohol and impure meat. This enabled them to withdraw from much Giriama social life and its accompanying drain on their funds, just as Jehovah's Witnesses could withdraw from unwanted matrilineal ties. By the 1960s, moreover, the accumulators were beginning to intermarry and thus create the group solidarity which was another potential advantage of minority status. Islam may also have facilitated their relations with the coastal business community, but Parkin's account does not bring out the practical advantages of this kind which Islam may have had for entrepreneurs.

For that aspect of Islam's relationship with capitalism we must turn to the long-standing Islamic culture of the West African savanna. There the association of business communities with particular Islamic brotherhoods is long established. By 1900, for example, all the North African traders in Zinder (in modern Niger) belonged to the Sanusi brotherhood, which enforced contracts among them and provided them with services all the way across the Sahara to Tripoli.[15] During the twentieth century somewhat similar patterns appeared among West Africans. One such innovation was the growth of the Reformed Tijaniyya, a brotherhood of Senegalese origin which was introduced to Kano in northern Nigeria in 1937 and was thought thirty years later to have gained the adherence of more than half the city's men. In Kano the Reformed Tijaniyya performed several functions. It reinforced the emirate's autonomy within the Sokoto Caliphate, whose official brotherhood was the rival Qadiriyya.

It encouraged a genuine spiritual earnestness and popular participation. It was more progressive than the Qadiriyya and provided a more effective base for resistance to westernisation. And its combination of openness to innovation with stress on ascetic dedication and individual responsibility made it especially attractive to the city's business community.[16] Outside Kano, the Hausa commercial community of Ibadan joined the Tijaniyya *en masse* in the 1950s, partly in order to reinforce their communal solidarity when threatened by competition from local Yoruba merchants.[17]

The second organisational innovation was the Wahhabi movement which first touched West Africa in the 1930s but became established after 1945, mainly in Bamako and other towns of modern Mali, through the teaching of local students returning from the Azhar university in Cairo.[18] Despite its name (given by its opponents), the movement had little to do with the Wahhabism of Arabia. It was essentially a West African version of the Salafiyya, the modernistic reforming movement within Islam which had come into being in Cairo in the late nineteenth century and had become increasingly puritan as it spread westwards into Africa.[19] In Bamako, Wahhabism won its strongest support among the wealthy kola traders, who welcomed its strong work-ethic, its justification of wealth as necessary to charity, its rationalising hostility to mysticism and superstition, its championing of nationalism and democracy, and its attempt to create an educational system which would be both modern, Islamic, and useful to those entering a commercial career.[20] Wahhabism was perhaps the religious movement most completely adapted to the emerging capitalism of postwar Africa.

Yet has there also been any Islamic equivalent of Albert Atcho, any attempt – however unconscious – to use Islam to reconcile the unprivileged to the inequalities and work relationships of capitalist society? It is possible that if the Reformed Tijaniyya in Kano were examined as a popular movement – and hitherto it has been studied only at the élite level – it might reveal some of these qualities. Another candidate, about which much more is known, might be the Mouride brotherhood of Senegal. There the clientage relationship between the wealthy Mouride sheikhs and their peanut-growing Wolof followers has a quality similar to Atcho's relationship to his patients, in that by preserving traditional Wolof clientage into the modern context of production for the world market, the brotherhood both enabled its members to evade the full consequences of capitalism and enabled capitalism to become established among the Wolof without head-on conflict with the pre-capitalist order. Jean Copans, from whom I take this analysis, is surely right to see the brotherhood as adapted to the transition from pre-capitalist to capitalist relations, just as Atcho's ministry was a transitional phenomenon, and once more the association between spiritual force and material prosperity was strong: 'The odour of sanctity in the Mouride leader's compound', according to Donal Cruise O'Brien, 'very often comes with a whiff of Lanvin or Chanel Number Five.' Moreover, the Mouride brotherhood has always had a powerful business wing and many of Senegal's richest men belong to it. It is arguable, indeed, that the brotherhood's main function is now to integrate rich and poor across the growing social divisions of Senegalese capitalism.[21] That too suggests parallels with Atcho's ministry, but Bregbo and the Mouride brotherhood were so totally different in scale and operation that the comparison must not be pressed too far. I do not know of any individual Muslim teacher performing functions comparable to Atcho's.

Nevertheless, African Islam offers almost as rich a variety of relationships between religious ideology and capitalist action as can be found within Christianity. That, however, does not by any means exhaust the range of Africa's religions. Have similar changes taken place within the indigenous religions of Africa? Have they too contributed ideologically and organisationally to the emergence of capitalism? This, emphatically, is still a subject for research. There is very little indication that indigenous religious institutions aided the emerging capitalist. Perhaps the only examples might be some of the quasi-secret societies of West Africa, notably that fascinating syncretic institution, the Reformed Ogboni Fraternity of southern Nigeria,[22] just as other businessmen of the West African coast have taken with alacrity to Freemasonry and the other fraternal societies of the European business world – thirteen of Liberia's nineteen presidents have been Freemasons, five of them Grand Masters.[23] Much more important, however, has been the capacity of African religions to ease the strains of social change resulting from the emergence of capitalism, much in the manner of Albert Atcho. Here the classic analysis is Margaret Field's study in the 1950s of the protection shrines of southern Ghana, whose proliferation she associated with the spread of cocoa growing. Field argued that commercialisation created insecurity for both the capitalist and the worker:

> Financially successful men are full of fear lest envious kinsmen should, by means of bad magic or witchcraft, bring about their ruin. Unsuccessful men are convinced that envious malice is the cause of their failure.[24]

Of the 2537 clients she studied, 397 complained that they were 'not prospering', including a disproportionate number from insecure occupations like lorry-driving.[25] On the other hand, a 'well-adjusted and serene man of Akwapim' told her:

> It is only since Tigari [a new shrine divinity] and the other protectors came that rich men in Akwapim have dared to show their riches by building big houses. Before that, if they did anything to show their wealth, they were sure to be killed.[26]

That was an exaggeration and there is little evidence of the viewpoint from elsewhere in Africa. But the use of indigenous religious resources by the unsuccessful in the modern economy is well-attested. In Tanzania, for example, workers from Dar es Salaam are known to travel one hundred miles to consult a renowned fertility shrine for medicine to 'wash the bad smell' which is thought to cause persistent unemployment.[27]

To this point the discussion has concentrated on how religious beliefs and institutions could facilitate the growth of African capitalism. It would be logical, however, to think that indigenous religious resources would be most effective in aiding resistance to that process. Yet precision is needed here. There is, of course, massive evidence of African resistance to European capitalism: violent opposition to land alienation, plantation strikes, and so on. The question is whether there is evidence of resistance to African capitalism and of religious bases for such resistance. The answer is probably more complicated than one might expect.

There is a valuable starting-point in a study of rural responses to capitalism in Colombia.[28] The author, Michael Taussig, argues that the Colombian rural poor think in terms of natural economy and use values. They regard money, of itself, as sterile, non-reproductive. Those for whom it does reproduce must therefore be using magic. One practice, it is thought, is secretly to introduce a banknote into a baptism ceremony so that the note rather than the baby is baptised; its owner prospers while the child is damned. Taussig's analysis prompts one to ask how Africans perceived capitalism when it first appeared amongst them – and it is when faced with such a question that one realises how little is really known about the thinking of rural Africans.

Perhaps in our present state of ignorance there are three points to be made about initial African perceptions of capitalism. One is that it was often associated in men's minds with witchcraft. Robert Harms has recently applied Taussig's analysis to the Bobangi traders who dominated the commerce of the middle Congo during the nineteenth century. Believing that the total sum of wealth was fixed, they saw commerce as a zero-sum game in which success could be won only by sacrifice – characteristically the sacrifice of a relative's life to the witches.[29] Such views were very common. Monica Wilson recorded in the 1930s that the most successful trader in the

Selya area of Tanzania was believed to owe his prosperity to a medicine hitherto used only by chiefs. Many rural Rhodesians were said in the 1960s to believe that a successful trader must have buried the heart of a close relative under his counter. The Sukuma people of northern Tanzania long ascribed the success of pioneer cotton farmers to the fact that they had made zombies work for them.[30] It was probably an indication of the different levels of capitalist development in the two societies that African witchcraft beliefs had a powerful levelling quality, whereas witchcraft accusations in early modern England were usually made by the more prosperous villagers against their poorer neighbours,[31] but recently something closer to the English pattern has appeared in Africa, presumably as a result of growing individualisation. From southwestern Tanzania, for example, there is evidence of successful farmers calling in witchfinders to persecute commercial rivals and of rich men taking positive advantage of a reputation for witchcraft. In August 1957 the people of a village in this region resolved to expel the wealthiest local farmer and enjoy his fourteen acres of river-valley land – but to no avail:

> Chomo had had wind of the intention of his enemies and was well prepared for the encounter. He worked himself into a trance-like state of inebriation and smeared ash over his face and chest to add ferocity to his countenance. He knew that people feared his sorcery and that he was reputed to have trained his cows for his malevolent practices.
>
> When the threatening mob of villagers had assembled around his houses, and began to shout that they would put fire to the thatched roofs, Chomo suddenly emerged from the byre chasing his cows in the direction of the mob. He followed behind spear in hand. Overwhelmed by this sight people panicked and ran for safety. Thereafter no more attempts were made to evict him forcibly.[32]

A second initial response to early African capitalism was the very common antipathy to working for wages for other members of one's own community. It was estimated in 1972 that less than 10 per cent of workers on Ghanaian cocoa farms were employed in their home areas.[33] Among the highly individualistic Baoule people of Ivory Coast young men were willing to migrate seasonally in order to work for Baoule of other regions or even for Baoule relatives who had themselves migrated to farm in other regions; what they would not do was to undertake paid labour for Africans in their own home area, for that was seen as demeaning.[34] Similar attitudes were found in many regions, especially perhaps in societies with egalitarian traditions or where slavery had been common.

Yet the third and much the most important point is that as a whole there was astonishingly little organised resistance to early African capitalism. There was resistance to proletarianisation, but apart from accusations of witchcraft – which had long been made against the successful and were by nature *ad hominem* – there simply is no evidence of co-ordinated hostility to, say, the emergent Ghanaian cocoa farmers before the First World War, although there was resistance by the populist *asafo* companies to chiefs who sold land to immigrant cocoa farmers for their own profit.[35] The only apparent exception may have been hostility by land-controlling authorities towards ambitious young planters – as on Kilimanjaro in Tanzania in the 1920s[36] – and the popular dissent in Buganda at the same period which was absorbed into the Bataka Movement, although it is not clear how far that movement expressed hostility to the growth of capitalism as such, given that the supposedly discontented peasants were at the same time beginning to acquire freehold ownership of land.[37] The lack of evidence of extensive hostility to early capitalists may, of course, be a result of ignorance, but I doubt it. I suspect that the reason lies partly in the response which Waddell's sermon in praise of bourgeois values evoked from the leading men of Old Calabar: 'they knew all that themselves already'. Most Africans were accustomed to a hedonistic pragmatism. Most were accustomed to considerable commercial exchange – the witchcraft accusations against rich men quoted from Tanzania all came from areas remote from the trade routes which crossed the country in the nineteenth century. More important, there was usually much leeway – in the form of vacant land and migrant labour – for individuals to acquire wealth without initially harming their neighbours. That was how what Marx called the syntheses of capitalist and pre-capitalist elements, so characteristic of rural Africa in this century, came to be formed. In responding to capitalism in this way, Africans displayed the same eclecticism as they showed in their responses to most other innovations of foreign origin – an eclecticism which was, of course, the logical corollary of pragmatism. In most areas of tropical Africa, for example, Western medicine has been accepted not as a substitute for indigenous medical practices but as a supplementary method of treating certain maladies for which experience has shown Western medicine to be efficacious.[38] Agricultural innovation has followed a similar pattern: new crops have been adopted where they have proved profitable and could be added to the existing agricultural cycle without disrupting it.[39] Initial responses to Islam and Christianity were commonly the same: their apparently useful elements were adopted into eclectic local religious systems.

In the case of religion, however, eclecticism did not always survive. Often there came a point at which Africans realised that unlike their old divinities, Allah and Jehovah were jealous gods and intolerant of eclecticism. This has been the point at which most of modern Africa's religious crises have taken place. West Africa's nineteenth-century jihads are the best example.[40] The same has been true of capitalism. Initially synthesised with pre-capitalist relationships, in certain cases it bred contradictions which came to the surface in resistance at the moment when a thoroughgoing capitalism – a genuine expropriation of means of production from the weaker members of society – threatened those comfortable syntheses of capitalist and pre-capitalist elements. From this perspective many of modern Africa's protest movements fall into a pattern. Two have already been mentioned: the element of agrarian protest in the Mau Mau rebellion of 1952 and the Zanzibar Revolution of 1964.[41] As further illustrations it is best to take two of the sub-continent's most turbulent peasant societies of recent years.

Most of the agrarian protest that has taken place in Nigeria since independence has occurred in Yorubaland. In large part it has been due to political factionalism and misgovernment, but it has contained also a strong element of hostility by peasant cocoa growers to the wealthy capitalist farmers and traders who increasingly dominated the countryside as the synthesis which Galletti had studied in 1951 broke down. In the Yoruba riots of 1965, according to Christopher Wrigley, it was these richer farmers 'who in practice bore the main brunt of popular anger. Cars, cocoa plantations and "better" houses were destroyed with the greatest zest.'[42] Three years later the more formidable Agbekoya Rebellion was launched mainly by Yorubaland's poor and middle peasants. Their victims again included rich farmers and Dr Eades has explained that one element in the background to the rebellion was growing indebtedness and inequality in the countryside.[43] During the last thirty years the common people of Yoruba towns (especially Ibadan) have shown similar antipathy to the growth of modern capitalism.[44]

The Yoruba have a long history of social protest and the frequency and effectiveness of their recent actions may owe much to the fact that their traditional moral economy survived through the colonial period, for colonial rule may well have been lighter in Yorubaland than anywhere else in the continent, with one exception. The exception, of course, was Ethiopia. The revolution that began in Ethiopia in 1974 and is still continuing has provided clear evidence of rural responses to the two stages of capitalist penetration into the countryside. As an enormous over-simplification, there were two main systems of land tenure in Ethiopia before the revolution. In the northern and central highlands, the core of the ancient kingdom, land was owned by amorphous bilateral descent groups and was distributed among their members by a complicated system of rights and bargains which generally enabled men to secure enough land to support their families, while permitting considerable inequality between individuals; from the produce of the land a tribute was paid to the state or an individual nobleman.[45] By contrast, southern Ethiopia and some outlying areas had been conquered only in the late nineteenth century and had been treated as conquered territory: most of the land had been seized and distributed to the victorious highlanders, the local peasants remaining as tenants paying one-third or even three-quarters of their crop.[46] From the end of the Second World War, the Ethiopian government, with strong foreign advice, gradually committed itself to the encouragement of rural capitalism as a necessary means of economic development. As Haile Sellassie said in 1961, 'The fundamental obstacle to the full realisation of the full measure of Ethiopia's agricultural potential has been, simply stated, lack of security in the land. . . . It is our aim that every Ethiopian should own his own land.'[47] In the densely populated north, land reform proposals met violent resistance, partly because they implied higher taxes and partly because they 'would convert a fluid system of individual inequalities into a permanent pattern of economic and social stratification'.[48] Gojjam province alone experienced three peasant revolts in the generation before the revolution. Nor were northern noblemen any more amenable to land reform than northern peasants, for a decree of 1966 abolishing private tribute was a dead letter. In the south and the peripheries, on the other hand, land was more easily available and the two decades before the revolution saw major changes in agriculture. Coffee developed as a cash-crop in certain regions, mechanised grain production flourished in others, and a number of foreign-financed agrobusiness enterprises took over large tracts of land. The result was the eviction of many thousands of tenants, their conversion into landless labourers, and the emergence of a growing number of capitalist entrepreneurs from the old privileged class.[49] Ethiopia before the revolution was an example of what rural capitalism might mean in Africa if sponsored by a regime unconstrained by democratic pressures or progressive ideology.

The Ethiopian Revolution has been predominantly an urban movement, but responses to it in the countryside have fallen very clearly into the pattern I am suggesting. During 1974 and 1975 southern tenants and labourers generally seized the land from their alien landlords, often driving them out, destroying some agricultural machinery, and then redistributing the land under the aegis of peasant associations. In the north, by contrast, although the new regime did at last abolish tribute, there was no peasant movement but rather a continuing suspicion of land reform.[50] Early in the revolution a northern peasant told an anthropologist: 'When I heard talk of agrarian reform, I thought: that will be well for the southern provinces, but here we have no need of it because we have always possessed our own land.'[51] In both north and south, however, there was a marked drop in the proportion of the crop that was marketed. As so often in modern Africa, the peasant associations soon came to be dominated by their most enterprising members, who sometimes began to emerge as kulaks. The military regime tried to resist this tendency and in 1979 it produced a scheme for a gradual movement towards producer co-operatives, but in 1980 there were only forty in existence.[52] Like Africa's other revolutions in Zanzibar and Rwanda, the Ethiopian Revolution has entrenched the peasants in the control of land. That control will not easily be broken.

The resistance to mechanised farming and agrobusiness schemes seen in southern Ethiopia has been paralleled in recent years in other parts of the continent, especially in the West African savanna where these schemes have especially been concentrated. The best-documented case is Jack Goody's account of the burning of crops and occasional destruction of agricultural machinery in northern Ghana in the late 1970s when soaring food prices and easy credit encouraged mechanised rice-farming in areas where commercial agriculture was previously little developed. Goody describes the rice-burners as 'the excluded: not the dispossessed so much as the non-joiners, the believers in traditional ways, the non-progressives'.[53] One is struck by the parallel with another violent resistance to modernity in the savanna: the so-called Maitatsine Rebellion of December 1980 in Kano city, when 4177 people are said to have died in riots initiated by a fundamentalist Islamic sect composed mainly of young rural immigrants and opposed not only to all kinds of westernisation – imported clothes, watches, cars – but to any form of education except study of the Koran.[54] Nor has such second-stage resistance been confined to West Africa. A less dramatic but particularly clear example comes from the recent history of religion in the Buganda kingdom.[55] From the 1930s Buganda's very powerful Protestant Church experienced a spiritual revival which not only permeated the church leadership but became deeply interwoven with Buganda's part-peasant, part-capitalist society. Sober, earnest, and inner-directed, many Revival brethren also became modestly prosperous in the things of this world – in 1951 the Principal of Makerere College observed how many of his students seemed to come from families to be found among the *balokole*, the 'saved ones'. In the 1950s, however, Buganda began to move into the second, more modern stage of capitalism, especially in trade and industry, just as it also moved into the larger world of the Ugandan national state. Catherine Robins has traced the reaction of the old Revival brethren against these new forms of material progress which were seen as corrupting the world they knew. The reaction began in 1960 and was known as the Reawakening (*Okuzukuka*). Its leaders were obsessed by the symbols of modern capitalism:

> The Lord gave us a cheque book . . . and signed cheque(s) too. You simply kneel down and say what you want in the name of Jesus Christ, our Lord, and the banks are opened. You simply take out the money with the cheques.[56]

Yet it was precisely these symbols of bourgeois society that the movement denounced: debt, life insurance, and those faithful companions of African capitalism, guard dogs.

This analysis of resistance to capitalism has focused on the defence of the old order, often by destructive methods reminiscent of Captain Swing.[57] But there are more creative and forward-looking ways of resisting capitalism. One with a long history in several continents is utopianism. There is a fascinating book waiting to be written on African utopias. Most have had religious inspiration, for almost every African religious leader, whatever his creed, seems compelled to create a cult centre or Zion or *jama'a* for his zealots. More recently there have been political utopias, from Cold Comfort Farm to Tanzania's *ujamaa* villages. There have even been capitalist utopias: the Lagos merchants tried to create one at Agege in the 1890s and African farmers in Natal did the same a generation earlier. But Africa's most interesting utopia has been Aiyetoro, the extraordinary combination of religious community and manufacturing centre founded in 1947 on the Nigerian coast, east of Lagos, by members of a local independent church.[58] In reaction against Nigeria's emerging postwar capitalism, Aiyetoro began as an authoritarian theocracy in which all property was held in common, work was done collectively for the profit of the whole community, and marriage was for a time abolished. But it also expressed the traditional work ethic which Waddell had stumbled upon a hundred years earlier. At Aiyetoro this was elaborated into a belief that hard work and prosperity were demonstrations of faith and assurances of salvation. These ideas dovetailed easily with the developmental ethos universal in postwar Nigeria. With such beliefs and such discipline, the community was immensely successful on an economic plane, establishing several factories and building nearly twenty large passenger boats and seven fully mechanised ocean-going trawlers. The success was its undoing. Collectivist discipline began to collapse, it appears, when the community as a whole hired workers from outside to help in its expanding industries. In 1968 private enterprise appeared among community members, followed by wage-payments, competition, differentiation, collapse of community spirit, economic decline, and emigration, leaving behind the remnants of a community functioning chiefly to the advantage of its former leaders, now turned wealthy private businessmen. Ironically, Aiyetoro is the ultimate illustration of the pervasiveness of capitalist values in modern Nigeria.

Within the socialist tradition, utopianism is seen as a cul-de-sac. Progress comes rather through struggle within the capitalist order. There is, of course, massive evidence of African workers resisting European capitalism through strikes, trade union activity, and the like. But is there evidence of African workers using such means to oppose African employers? This raises a central problem of the next lecture: our ignorance of how modern, African-owned enterprises function. But there is one such body of evidence in Paul Lubeck's account of labour relations in Kano in northern Nigeria, where African employers were more prominent than perhaps in any other city in the continent. Lubeck visited Kano twice, in 1971 and 1975.[59] In 1971 there were no trade unions in the city's factories, since the employers had vetoed them. African factory-owners, especially, practised a paternalistic style of management with a relaxed work-discipline of the kind often reported in Third World factories; in these enterprises the workers' consciousness was especially low. When most of Nigeria's factory workers struck in 1971 to enforce the payment of a national wage award, Kano's African employers successfully resisted the pressure. Lubeck describes one locking out his whole labour force for several weeks before bringing them to heel with little violence. By 1975, however, much had changed. Kano's industrial sector had grown rapidly. Inflation had cut sharply into earnings. Workers had learned from the experience of the earlier strike. And by reorganising the labour movement on a national scale, the government had unwittingly extended it to Kano's factories for the first time. 'Our eyes have been opened', workers declared. So when employees struck again in 1975 to enforce a wage award, Kano's factory workers acted perhaps even more vigorously against African employers than against aliens, denouncing the African capitalists 'for not recognising the needs of their countrymen during a period of high inflation'. As that statement suggests, full class consciousness was still a long way off, but the development over the four-year period was very striking. And Lubeck observed that those workers who had the most Islamic training and were most active in religious brotherhoods were also the most militant in industrial disputes. Islam, he thought, had the same effect in encouraging labour activity in Kano as Methodism is traditionally said to have had in Britain.

This is a fitting place to end a lecture which began by considering religion as capitalism's ally and has ended by examining it as capitalism's enemy. For my aim has been to show the great diversity of connections between ideologies and the emergence of African capitalism. And Kano, too, is the right place to end such a lecture, for Kano is the historic focus of African capitalism. It was the growth-point in the nineteenth century. And it is today again the spearhead of the new urban capitalism which has accompanied African independence.

4   Capitalists and Politicians

I began these lectures by asking whether African capitalists have been able to establish themselves as a creative force in their societies and, if so, whether their capitalism has taken distinctive forms when compared with other continents. This last lecture will consider the development of urban capitalism in Africa since the Second World War, especially the growth of manufacturing industry. It will ask whether the characteristics and problems of urban capitalism can be understood by considering it as a late capitalism, late to appear in the global history of capitalism, using in particular Alexander Gerschenkron's comparative analysis of industrial revolutions.[1] Gerschenkron argued that each industrial revolution differed from its predecessors precisely because it came later. The later a country industrialised, the greater was the gap separating it from the most advanced economies of the time. The later a country industrialised, therefore, the more discontinuous, traumatic, and politically directed was its industrial revolution. Gerschenkron restricted his analysis to Europe and Japan. I do not wish to suggest that an industrial revolution has yet begun in any tropical African country, but I do want to ask whether Gerschenkron's approach can advance our understanding of modern African urban capitalism and whether African experience can contribute to the comparative study of industrialisation.

In tropical Africa, modern industry mainly dates from the Second World War,[2] when several circumstances came together to change the old pattern of exported raw materials and imported manufactures. Colonial governments sought to diversify economies, local European settlers aimed to achieve greater economic autonomy, and competing international companies tried to outflank their rivals by establishing subsidiaries in the colonies behind protective tariff barriers, while the increasing use of synthetics in many manufacturing processes also encouraged a movement from primary production into industry.[3] In 1950, for example, Nigeria's manufacturing sector still provided only 0.45 per cent of GNP, the smallest proportion of any country in the world producing statistics,[4] but during the 1950s the value of manufacturing output grew nearly five times, as former importers competed to establish subsidiaries.[5] In 1970 manufacturing provided 9.5 per cent of Nigeria's GNP.[6] During the 1970s manufacturing output grew in real terms at an annual average of 12–13 per cent, although growth has been more irregular since 1979.[7] Its size and oil wealth make Nigeria an extreme case, but a similar postwar growth of manufacturing took place on a smaller scale in most of the richer countries of tropical Africa.[8] It is noteworthy that Africa's first modern manufacturing enterprises were often started by foreign firms, whereas in Latin America the earliest import-substitution industries were generally founded by local businessmen and were dominated by foreign firms only two or three decades later.[9] This was one consequence for Africa of being a late starter in the development of capitalism. Nevertheless, in the richer countries of tropical Africa local businessmen have since independence obtained a growing share in the development of urban enterprise.

During the 1960s and early 1970s a number of researchers examined the social origins of African businessmen. They found that entrepreneurs had come from four kinds of background, depending on the enterprises concerned and the particular histories of different countries. In West Africa small manufacturers had often emerged from the traditional artisan sector, especially in the metal-working trades, furniture-

making, and allied industries.[10] Very rarely had these
craftsmen possessed the skills or the desire to create anything
but a very small firm.[11] In eastern and southern Africa, by
contrast, the artisan sector had been dominated by aliens and
had therefore less often been a source of African entrepreneurs;
instead, many pioneer African industrialists had previously
worked in foreign-owned firms in the same trade, a pattern
rare in West Africa.[12] On the whole, however, the larger
African firms of the 1960s were not owned by men with
technical experience. Many of the more successful
industrialists had been traders who had moved into
production, a pattern found everywhere in the Third World.
This emerged especially clearly from Peter Kilby's study of the
Nigerian baking industry, much the best account of African
entrepreneurship yet written and a model for the industrial
histories which are so much needed. Kilby showed that many
of the most successful Nigerian bakers had been traders and
that they were especially skilful at marketing, as might be
expected in a society so dedicated to trade.[13] In the same way,
timber contractors had set up saw mills and rubber traders had
gone into rubber processing.[14] Again, however, this had been a
pattern mainly confined to West Africa because of alien
domination of commerce elsewhere, so that most of the larger
entrepreneurs in eastern and southern Africa were educated
men who had moved out of white-collar employment. When an
African Chamber of Commerce had been formed in
Johannesburg in 1955, for example, six of the eleven members
of its executive had been former schoolteachers.[15] A study of the
wealthiest African businessmen in Lusaka in 1970 found that
they had characteristically 'entered business directly from the
better jobs that were open to Africans in the colonial era'.
Seventy per cent had fathers who had been employed in the
cash economy; 65 per cent had more than six years of
education.[16] In other words, they were characteristically
products of the straddling process which had also been the
main source of rural capitalists in eastern and southern Africa.
Yet some West African entrepreneurs of the 1960s also had

white-collar backgrounds of this kind, although less predominantly than in the east and south. In Nigeria several civil servants and professional men had moved into business, normally as merchants but occasionally as industrialists. The most successful printing works in Lagos in the mid-1960s were owned by former clerks and civil servants; together with certain very modern import-substitution industries they were the most profitable industrial enterprises owned by Africans in the whole Lagos region.[17]

Thus during the 1960s and early 1970s the origins of African entrepreneurship revealed a strong contrast between West Africa, with its long-established capitalistic sector and its entrepreneurs from artisanship and trade, and eastern and southern Africa, where entrepreneurs had emerged chiefly through the straddling process of Western education and modern sector employment. The other general pattern, most evident in West Africa, was that the contrast between the craftsman-entrepreneur (who tended to remain a small producer) and the trader-entrepreneur (who was often more expansive) was beginning to be over-ridden by the emergence of a third type of industrialist, who was often a well-educated man with managerial or administrative experience at a high level.[18] Since the early 1970s this trend appears to have continued, so far as one can judge from the very limited recent research on the subject. When Dr Idemudia surveyed 101 of Nigeria's larger African industrialists in 1975, he found that 60 per cent had at least secondary education, that 68 per cent had previously been business employees – a marked reversal of earlier patterns – and that there was a negative correlation between entrepreneurial success and birth into a family with a business tradition.[19] All this suggested that as Nigerians created larger and more modern enterprises, so experience in older economic spheres became irrelevant and only the higher levels of education and employment experience in modern fields became useful. So attractive was private business to high-level administrative personnel that in 1979 the Nigerian government temporarily prohibited permanent secretaries from moving into the private sector. Similar trends were noted in Ghana and Zambia during the 1970s, while Kenya met the problem by allowing civil servants to run businesses while keeping their official posts.[20]

This changing pattern of entrepreneurship is exactly what a model of late industrialisation or late capitalism would predict. It is worth pursuing the point further into the data on African business practices which were collected by the many studies made in the 1960s. These studies were often highly critical. Left-wing critics denounced African businessmen as both exploitative and dependent, as mere front-men for foreign capitalists. Liberal critics complained that the entrepreneurs were simply inadequate as businessmen. To all this the entrepreneurs replied by recounting their rags-to-riches stories, by stressing the asceticism of their lives (sometimes with justification), and by enumerating the obstacles they had surmounted. It is the obstacles and the means of surmounting them that should interest us.

Businessmen themselves generally insisted that their chief obstacle was shortage of capital, for which they blamed especially the unhelpfulness of expatriate banks. African academics generally agreed with them, whereas expatriate researchers concluded that capital was more easily available than competent entrepreneurs with viable projects. The argument reached no agreement and has probably now been outdated by the development of indigenous financial institutions, but it has revealed that banks and other institutions have not yet played the entrepreneurial role in the growth of manufacturing which they filled, for example, in late-industrialising Germany.[21] It was still true in the 1970s that most initial capital employed by African businessmen came from private savings or relatives – although some of the bigger firms were launched with institutional loans – and that further capital for extension came overwhelmingly from reinvested profits.[22] This, however, introduced another and potentially more serious obstacle to the growth of African capitalism: the easy availability in modern Africa of alternative investment opportunities which were more profitable but less productive than manufacturing industry. When Samir Amin wrote his critique of capitalism in Ivory Coast in the 1960s, one reason he gave for the non-existence of a developing African capitalism there was the tendency for wealthy Ivoirians to invest both in agriculture and in such safe and rewarding fields as urban property.[23] For businessmen to seek status and security by investing in property – 'the treason of the bourgeoisie', as Braudel calls it[24] – has been regarded as an obstacle to industrial growth everywhere from Britain to China. Modern Africa has seen periods when capital was invested predominantly in agriculture, as during the cash-crop boom at the beginning of this century, and other times when the main object of investment was urban property. Given the massive urbanisation which the continent has experienced in this century, the history of urban property markets is clearly of great importance, but the first studies of this subject are only just beginning to appear.[25] They suggest that urban property has generally been both a more secure investment than trade or industry, easier to finance by means of loans from banks or the state, and simply more profitable. It was reckoned in the 1960s that capital invested in house-building in the low-income area of Mathare Valley in Nairobi could be wholly recovered in rent in eighteen months.[26] For Nairobi's African bourgeoisie in recent years – as in the past for Europeans and Indians – property ownership has been described accurately as the 'express lift to prosperity'.[27] Of course, this was not necessarily unproductive investment, especially given its linkages to the construction industry. Nor was it in any sense contrary to accumulation or capitalist rationality, for capitalism is about profit, not progress. But there was nevertheless truth in Samir Amin's claim that this alternative outlet for capital checked the development of African capitalism in that it encouraged rentier rather than productive activity.

Peter Garlick, who described Ghanaian businessmen in the 1960s as 'rentiers at heart',[28] believed that the chief obstacle to their advancement lay in African social structures, especially the burden of supporting an extended family. Of 62 Ghanaian traders whom Garlick interviewed around 1960, 38 said that they were each educating at least six children and one was an only son responsible for 29 sisters. Keith Hart has described another Ghanaian entrepreneur whose income of some £20,000 a year supported 11 wives, 17 children, and 'a floating household of 80 persons'.[29] Yet in a sense these were the fruits of success for those who chose to express it in the traditional manner of clientelism. Other studies have found that businessmen generally managed to keep their kinship obligations within reasonable limits.[30] 'In business one has no mother and father', says a Kikuyu proverb. What is clear is that business success in the twentieth century, as in the nineteenth, required a capacity to manipulate both the traditional and the modern worlds. That social structures were not a crucial obstacle to capitalist success was probably evidenced by the fact that the capitalists did not usually come from marginal social groups, although there was a strong tendency for particular ethnic communities to produce disproportionately large numbers of entrepreneurs, generally because of privileged access to modern advantages, the absence of alternative career opportunities, and the existence of the supportive institutions which grew up with entrepreneurial experience; the Ijebu Yoruba of Nigeria and the Kwahu and Frafra of Ghana were especially prominent in this way.[31] Moreover, as we have seen, there was a tendency for those who had become entrepreneurs to separate themselves in other ways, like the Lala of Zambia who became Jehovah's Witnesses or the Giriama entrepreneurs of Kenya who became Muslims.

A survey of Nigerian entrepreneurs in the 1960s showed that although they said their own major problem was lack of capital, they said the major problem of *other* entrepreneurs was bad management.[32] Virtually all studies of African industrialists have agreed that the quality of management was the most important reason for their success or failure. Although the technological innovation they carried out was meagre, since they were essentially importers of foreign technology, nevertheless the organisational innovation required to create a modern firm was very great indeed, especially for a manufacturing firm, partly because modern production processes were simply so much more complicated than they had been in eighteenth-century England and partly because the models of large-scale economic activity in African societies – cash-crop farms, trading caravans, weaving compounds, and the like – were little guide to factory management because they did not organise *divided* labour.[33] Of the many topics in the history of African capitalism that need research, the study of how African entrepreneurs have managed their enterprises is perhaps the most important. The problem of managing factories has been a bottleneck in the early stage of every industrialisation. To meet it, businessmen of different nationalities have tried to mobilise every resource available. Early British factory-owners used the non-economic device of contracts to limit the freedom of their workers and often employed pauper children because no other workers could be induced.[34] The early Indian and Chinese textile industries used sub-contractors (known as 'jobbers') to hire and control labour and practised an internal work-discipline which was less rigorous than in Europe, since the vital thing was to ensure that the very expensive machinery characteristic of late industrialisation was kept in operation all the time by someone.[35] Japanese textile mills, by contrast, regimented their girl employees in an extraordinarily paternalistic way, offered them training in cooking, sewing, music, flower-arranging, and the tea ceremony, and occasionally even found them husbands.[36] In the light of these devices, it would be particularly interesting to know how African entrepreneurs have faced the same difficulties and whether they too have used culture-specific expedients. Lubeck's study of Kano, for example, suggests that some African managers tolerated a more relaxed work-discipline than Europeans and that supervisors had some functions similar to those of jobbers in India, although modern technology makes the full model of early Indian factory organisation impossible today. Margaret

Peil found that Ghanaian factory workers had difficulty in observing time-discipline and deeply resented close supervision by foremen whom they condemned as 'too enthusiastic'.[37] It has been suggested that close factory supervision is most easily accepted in strongly hierarchical societies like those of eastern Asia.[38] If that is true, the outlook for African production management is bleak. Another disturbing point is that African managers, when interviewed, have often expressed contempt for the quality of their workers.[39] Research in these fields would probably tell us a great deal about contemporary African capitalism.

Yet the problem is more complicated than this. African industrial capitalism is not merely African capitalism, it is late capitalism. In a comparative study of British and Japanese industry, Professor Dore has shown that the Japanese system of organisation-orientated labour relations – intense company loyalty, promotion by strict seniority, enveloping paternalism – came into being not simply because Japan had paternalistic traditions but also because Japan was a late industrialiser.[40] This had three consequences: industrialists faced problems, such as training workers from scratch to operate modern and expensive machinery, which could be met only by high levels of labour stability and discipline; industrialists enjoyed advantages not available to their British predecessors, such as the possibility of recruiting their workers from the ablest pupils in a state education system; and, above all, Japanese industrialists were able and were obliged to imitate the most modern management practices of the late nineteenth and early twentieth centuries. One of the pioneers of paternalism in the Japanese textile industry later declared that he 'found the inspiration for many of his plans ·in Krupp and the National Cash Register Corporation'.[41] From this analysis Professor Dore has formulated a series of propositions about late industrialisation which deserve to be set alongside Gerschenkron's original hypotheses. Dore suggests that the later a country industrialises, the less its industrialists will be guided by laissez-faire ideology; the more likely are industrial personnel to have passed through a modern school system; the bigger will be the technological and organisational leaps that have to be made; the more rational and bureaucratic will be the initial patterns of industrial organisation; the sooner will management concern itself with workers' welfare and recognise trade union rights; and the more will trade unions be enterprise-based and job-protective. Dore suggests that these propositions might apply to all late-industrialising countries. Recent studies of labour relations in modern African factories give only partial support to his theories. Contemporary African factory workers generally are educated young men anxious to protect their much-coveted jobs and willing to spend a decade or more in a single enterprise, but their goal is usually to save enough to establish themselves as independent businessmen.[42] The relatively high wages paid by modern manufacturing firms in Kenya did help to domesticate the trade union movement, while in Nigeria company unions have been fairly common and some have been anything but militant.[43] Yet the more normal pattern in Africa has been industrial unionism and there is evidence that modern factory workers have often been among the more militant workers, partly because they were educated, partly because they found organisation relatively easy, and partly because their aim was to maximise their earnings in order to quit factory work entirely.[44] Africa is still a continent of land and opportunity, as it was in the nineteenth century, and African workers are not yet the lifelong company men of the Japanese stereotype, so that Professor Dore's propositions must be qualified to meet specific African circumstances. That may be equally true of his generalisations with regard to management, but we know too little about industrial management in Africa to be able to discuss them.

During the 1960s, critics of African businessmen invariably complained that entrepreneurs were incapable of delegating authority but instead ran one-man businesses which could not expand without collapsing in disorder. The one-man proprietorship was indeed the norm: 75 per cent of larger Ghanaian private firms studied in the late 1960s, for example, and 72 of 81 leading African businessmen in South Africa in the early 1970s.[45] There were many reasons for this. As pioneers, African businessmen were natural individualists and were often mistrustful, especially where their environment was insecure. As one told an investigator in Kenya, 'African businessmen, if they employ a person who has got experience, they don't trust him very much, because they are always so suspicious about money. That comes from poverty.'[46] There was in any case no cadre of professional managers to employ; one careful study considered this 'perhaps the major bottleneck to indigenous industrialisation'.[47] The result, as Samir Amin wrote of Senegal in 1969, was that 'Senegalese enterprises do not yet exist; only the entrepreneurs who have created them exist. The premature disappearance of an individual almost always entails that of the business.'[48] Most sole proprietorships everywhere in the world disappear at the proprietor's death.[49] In Africa there were added reasons why they should, notably the custom for sons to strike out independently at marriage and the fact that many inheritance systems were inimical to the continuity of firms – it is virtually impossible to imagine how a sole proprietorship could often survive its owner's death in a matrilineal society.

These problems give a special interest to those firms which have passed intact to a second generation, but very little is known about this. Businessmen in several countries have adopted European models of company formation, but there has rarely yet been time to see whether the companies can survive their founders. A study of the Lagos area in 1965 found that those second-generation Nigerian-owned industries still extant were incorporated firms and 'had remained essentially static',[50] but there have been very successful family firms in Lagos and western Nigeria and it is unfortunate that we know less about modern Yoruba capitalism than any other major instance in the continent. Probably the only large businesses known to have survived into a second generation have been some of the family firms of Kano in northern Nigeria[51] – once more, as in the nineteenth century, the vanguard of African capitalism, not only in this field but also in moving from trade into modern manufacturing. The reasons for this advance in Kano probably include the fact that the city's trade survived the early colonial period relatively unscathed, that its community of North African merchants provided a model of commercial organisation, and that many of the leading African business families began as kola merchants, a highly skilled trade in which family continuity has been especially marked: when Paul Lovejoy studied 150 kola traders in Kano in 1970, he found that 129 were grandsons of kola traders.[52] Whatever the reason, of the 20 largest Nigerian-owned manufacturing firms which Dr Idemudia studied in 1975, no less than 19 were in the north. He also found that northern firms were more willing to employ expatriate managers and that 70 per cent of all the firms he studied said that they recruited managers through formal procedures.[53] In this area, too, African businesses seem to have moved closer to the rational organisations characteristic of late industrialisation during the 1970s.

I have been considering the criticisms of African businessmen made chiefly by those who regarded them as inadequate capitalists. Criticism from the left, by contrast, focused more on the environment within which they worked, arguing that an autonomous and creative African capitalism was simply impossible because of the dominance of competing international firms and the hostility of the political environment. It is certainly true that African entrepreneurs faced intense competition. From one side they were squeezed by low-cost craft producers and the informal sector, from the other by state-owned industries or by foreign companies with superior access to imported technology and often with special privileges like tax exemptions granted by African governments which thought they were thereby encouraging industrialisation. As a result, African entrepreneurs generally operated in a border area between petty producers and foreign firms, an area – one thinks of saw-milling, furniture-making, baking, building materials, motor transport, and the like – where the capital requirements for entry were fairly low and

the technology relatively simple, with the result, of course, that
the competition among African entrepreneurs was intense.[54]
On the other hand, detailed studies showed that African
businessmen were probably less dependent on foreign capital
than was commonly believed. In import-export trade, of
course, the true comprador could still flourish, but the transfer
of much manufacturing from metropolitan countries into their
former colonies since 1945 meant a more competitive
relationship between foreign and local capital than at similar
stages of economic development in Asia or Latin America.[55]
Paul Kennedy's study of Ghanaian businessmen in the late
1960s showed that manufacturers preserved a fairly high
degree of autonomy and an even greater desire for it.[56] In
Kenya, where the desire for autonomy was equally strong, it
was nevertheless the view of the shrewd and strongly
nationalistic Kenyans in the Treasury that there was more to
be gained by co-operation with international capital than by
conflict with it.[57] (Although Njenga Karume's Tiger Shoe
Company aspires to supplant Bata, I noticed in the western
Kenyan town of Kericho in 1980 that the shop selling Tiger
Shoes, close to the Bata shop, was called Mini-Bata.) The
successful industrialists of Kano, similarly, had particularly
close partnership arrangements with foreign firms, sometimes
from economically efficient but politically powerless countries
like Taiwan. In May 1981 Nigeria's Minister of State for
Industry 'advised indigenous investors to pool their resources
and seek technical partnerships overseas so they could start
sound manufacturing enterprises'.[58] It is archaic to assume an
automatic hostility between international capital and national
capitalism, at least in favoured countries which are seen in the
West as nuclei of capitalism and political alliance within the
Third World.

In the relations between local and foreign capital, the role of
the state has been crucial. Everywhere in Africa the practical
problems of government – bureaucratic inefficiency and
obstruction, foreign exchange shortages, corruption and the
like – have been major obstacles to entrepreneurial success. But

very much more important to the businessman has been the overall government policy towards private African capitalism. This, of course, is a universal fact of life in the modern world. Professor Fieldhouse's recent study concluded that in all the underdeveloped countries in which Unilever operated, the main determinant of its profits was government policy; the company was the subordinate in its relationship with the state even when the company was Unilever and the state was the Solomon Islands.[59] It is well to remember the first principle for operating in Africa attributed to Lonrho, which ought to know: 'Even if your man out there is doing a first-class job and he falls foul of the government, then he must go.'[60] In Africa the role of the state has been especially vital, partly because no other institutions, such as the banks, have been willing to take the initiative in a late and indigenous industrialisation, and partly because Africa's modern private sector emerged at exactly the same moment as its nationalist politicians gained power, whereas in India, for example, modern capitalism was well entrenched before the colonial era ended. Relationships between businessmen and governments have therefore been particularly crucial in Africa since the 1950s.

As a very broad generalisation, three kinds of relationships between capitalists and politicians have emerged: three ideal types in Weber's sense, with some countries approximating very closely to one or other model and others combining elements from more than one. The first model is the regime which has sought to prevent the emergence of private African capitalism in any form. One example of this approach was Nkrumah's Ghana, especially in the last five years of his rule before his overthrow in 1966. Nkrumah believed that private enterprise was incapable of modernising Ghana at the breakneck speed which he envisaged. He feared, according to a senior adviser, 'that if he permitted African business to grow, it will grow to the extent of becoming a rival power to his and the party's prestige'.[61] Moreover, within the Convention People's Party were many men anxious to use state power to channel the economy's surplus in their own direction. It followed that although Nkrumah never attempted to nationalise foreign enterprises he deliberately confined local capitalism to small-scale operations while building up a massively expensive state sector – by 1965 the Minister of Finance was doctoring the figures for planned expenditure in order to convince Nkrumah that the government was spending more than it really was.[62] During the last twenty years the burden of supporting the overdeveloped state and its public enterprises has very largely ruined Ghana's productive economy.

Ghana is a special case because it was a relatively wealthy colony poised for capitalist development until turned in the opposite direction, almost entirely by the will of one man. By contrast, the other governments that have deliberately opposed local capitalism have generally ruled poor countries where few modern African capitalists existed to resist professedly socialist policies: Guinea, Mali in the 1960s under Modibo Keita, Benin, Congo-Brazzaville, Angola, Mozambique, Somalia, and above all Tanzania, which, after Nkrumah's fall, became the model of African socialism.

In the colonial period the wealthier regions of Tanzania developed tropical Africa's characteristic synthesis of peasant-and-capitalist society. After independence in 1961 the capitalist element advanced, especially where the bigger farmers had access to state resources and tractors. As President Nyerere said in retrospect:

> Capitalism was beginning. And it was beginning with the leadership. Certainly it was a mean and unproductive kind of capitalism which was beginning in Tanzania, but it was capitalism all the same.[63]

Nyerere's moral objection to capitalism merged with his belief that it was incapable of developing Tanzania and with many forces within the political system: the ambitions of officials and younger party members with no stake in the emerging capitalist sector, the demands of the poorer regions, the inadequacy of foreign aid, the general impatience for change,

and the weakness of capitalist vested interests. The outcome
was Tanzania's socialist programme of 1967 and the attempt to
reconstruct rural society on the basis of socialist villages.[64] At
present it is impossible to judge how successful this programme
has been, partly for lack of evidence, partly because it is
impossible to separate the consequences of rural socialism from
those of drought, oil price increases, low producer prices, and
the war against General Amin. But four generalisations may be
possible. First, since Independence Tanzania has seen a
massive expansion of peasant society: that is, an expansion of
commodity production, literacy, primary schooling,
elementary public hygiene, world religions, and the other
characteristics of peasant status to the enormous areas which
they had not penetrated during the colonial period. Second,
Tanzania's peasants have shown almost no enthusiasm for
rural socialism, except occasionally as a temporary step
towards individual accumulation. Third, many of the nuclei of
rural capitalism which existed in the mid-1960s were destroyed
during the next decade. The tractor-cultivated maize farms of
Ismani were officially expropriated on 11 May 1971 and almost
all the other private tractor-farming enterprises created in the
1950s and 1960s seem to have disappeared, although African-
owned plantations of tree-crops dating from the 1920s appear
to have survived better[65] – an interesting example of the greater
vulnerability of 'second-stage' rural capitalism suggested in the
previous lecture. Fourth, a great deal of small-scale rural
capitalism still exists in trade, transport, urban food supply,
the use of seasonal labour, and other fields where the
entrepreneurs are small enough to go through the eye of
the government's needle.[66] In 1977 Nyerere claimed that the
previous ten years had 'stopped, and reversed, a national drift
towards the growth of a class society'.[67] That such a drift has
been checked is probably true; that it has been reversed is not
yet clear. African governments have shown that they can
prevent capitalism; they have not yet shown that they can
replace it with anything else that will release their people's
energies.

If the first model of relationships between governments and capitalists has been the prevention of private enterprise, the second might be described as parasitic capitalism: that is, the use of state power to acquire private property and business interests, so that the holders of office are also the owners of property. To see parasitic capitalism at its most luxuriant we should probably look at Zaire. Because of the instability that accompanied its independence Zaire has been especially dependent on foreign aid, its political leadership has relied more than usual on coercion, its economy in the colonial period was particularly dominated by aliens and the urban sector, and its political instability has encouraged meteoric careers and a particularly brash and cynical materialism. A pamphlet by Tshitenji-Nzembele, *Devenez riche rapidement*, catches the mood. 'A man is more of a man when he has more wealth', he writes. Success depends on 'liberating the mind of all doubts as to the legitimacy of material wealth'. 'You must love money and pursue it tirelessly', he insists. 'Love money to distraction, adore it in thought and deed. It will end by coming to you', for 'God is incontestably a God of abundance.'[68] It is a fascinating modern version of Africa's old hedonistic pragmatism. And it is acted on. During Zaire's first fifteen years of independence the words used to describe its élite changed first from '*évolués*' to 'intellectuals', then to 'citizens', and finally to 'acquirers'.[69] The acquirers were the politicians and administrators who profited from the Zairianisation measures of 1973 and 1974 by which virtually all the foreign-owned enterprises in the country were transferred into the hands of some 2000 Zairians, although the resulting political anger and economic chaos led to many being returned and others nationalised.[70] It was among the political leaders who benefited from such measures that the great fortunes were made, but it should be stressed that a more productive capitalism on a smaller scale has also been growing up in Zaire beneath the flagrant corruption of 'the people of Nazareth and Bethlehem', as they are known in Kinshasa.[71]

Other countries approximate to this model of parasitic capitalism. One, Zambia, has managed to combine parts of it with elements of privately owned productive enterprise, a large state sector, and a good deal of socialist rhetoric in an extraordinary political balancing-act.[72] Moreover, parasitic capitalism can be used as a base from which to launch a more independent and productive form of private enterprise; that happened in Liberia during the last years of Tubman's presidency and the brief period of Tolbert's, and it is by no means clear that the military coup of 1980 has reversed the process.[73] But the interesting country from this viewpoint is Ivory Coast. Since 1950 Ivory Coast has experienced very rapid economic growth, partly through the exploitation of virgin forest for cash-crop agriculture (much as Ghana did before the First World War) and partly through the development of light import-substitution industry (as elsewhere in tropical Africa in recent decades). Between 1960 and 1979 the volume of industrial output grew at over 15 per cent a year.[74] This growth has been achieved in an open economy of a strongly capitalist character. But whether the result has been the creation of either a class of private Ivoirian capitalists or the conditions for one is much disputed. It is true that the share of foreign investment in the modern sector has declined over the period; in 1978 it was 46 per cent. But only 7 per cent of modern sector investment then came from private Ivoirian sources. The remaining 47 per cent was provided by the state.[75] Ivory Coast, it appears, may have moved from the predominance of European capitalism to that of state capitalism. One area of private Ivoirian capitalism has been cash-crop farming, but there is much dispute as to whether accumulation is still continuing in the countryside. Some believe that it does continue in the pioneer areas; Baoule migrant farmers are building villas in their home towns today as Akwapim did in Ghana eighty years ago.[76] Others think that the rural surplus is indeed channelled into the towns, into state investment, and especially into the pockets of a parasitic bourgeoisie whose wealth and business interests derive from their political and administrative positions.[77] The weakness of private Ivoirian capitalism in industry and commerce has several roots. One major reason is simply the country's dedication to growth at all costs and by means of an open economy, which has entrenched foreign interests and prevented their indigenisation or any effective schemes to aid private capital. A survey made in 1971 found only five Ivoirian industrial entrepreneurs, while a decade later three-quarters of Ivory Coast's trade was still in the hands of foreigners.[78] Another important reason has been the government's concern to embrace all sections of the community and to avoid identification as the political embodiment of the indigenous bourgeoisie. 'What the Ivory Coast will not know and must not know, in its own interest, is Ivoirian capitalism', President Houphouet-Boigny insisted shortly after Independence. 'The only capitalism that we must construct is that of the Ivoirian state.'[79] In 1979 the ruling party echoed him in a statement epitomising this blandest of regimes: 'There are no differentiated classes and no nascent bourgeoisie in Ivory Coast.'[80]

This hesitation contrasts sharply with the third model in the spectrum of relationships between governments and capitalists, a model which Sayre Schatz has aptly labelled 'nurture capitalism'.[81] By this he means a deliberate attempt by the state to create an economy in which at least substantial areas of enterprise would be in the hands of private capitalists. Such a deliberate – and therefore very remarkable – attempt to devolve eonomic power might result from an overlap of interests between government and private businessmen or from an ideological commitment to capitalism, but historically the most common and important motive for nurture capitalism has probably been nationalism. The belief that it was the most expedient means to achieve rapid national modernisation lay behind both the classic cases of nurture capitalism in recent history: late nineteenth-century Japan and mid twentieth-century South Africa. Nationalism is also at the heart of tropical Africa's two current experiments in nurture capitalism, in Kenya and Nigeria.

The two countries exemplify the two alternative paths to African capitalism. Nigeria typifies the West African model, growing out of a pre-colonial capitalistic sector of exchange which survived the colonial impact more successfully than elsewhere, while Kenya illustrates the predominant pattern of eastern and southern Africa, where Africans have sought to take over capitalist structures created by immigrant businessmen. Yet both have adopted similar national policies favouring mixed economies. In both countries private businessmen sporadically criticise the scale of state intervention in the economy; in Nigeria there is at present a major and very interesting debate on where the line between the private and the public sectors should be drawn.[82] Yet both there and in Kenya the growth of the private sector has in fact depended heavily on 'nurture' by the government, as has of course been the chief characteristic of late industrialising countries.

Thus in Kenya it was chiefly state finance that enabled Africans to buy European farms in the early 1960s. It was legislation that enabled them to take over much wholesale and retail trade from Asians. Kenya's African businessmen, unlike their European and Asian competitors, have obtained their loan capital chiefly from the state. In the 1970s government began to exercise control over foreign investment in manufacturing, which had hitherto been given almost free rein, and encouraged foreign companies to sell minority shareholdings to Kenyan citizens.[83] 'Ours is a mixed economy', President Daniel arap Moi told Parliament in March 1982, 'and it will be found, as we go on, that more and more private sector activities in manufacturing and other modern enterprises are in Kenyan hands. I want to stress that Kenyanisation is one of the government's important objectives and, indeed, strategies in our development efforts.'[84] Above all, the Kenyan state succeeded in releasing the ambitions and energies of very large numbers of its citizens and it guaranteed them a system of law and a structure of society in which the system of free wage-labour could be expanded.[85] In a global perspective these are perhaps the utterly indispensable conditions for the growth of capitalism.

Nigeria's policies were very similar, but its indigenisation programme has been more extensive and dramatic because oil revenues made it possible in the 1970s to insist on a massive

transfer of shareholdings in foreign companies to Nigerian
citizens. Figures are contradictory, but a conservative estimate
would be that over 200,000 Nigerians acquired shares in this
way. The United Africa Company alone disposed of shares to
75,450 applicants.[86] Those who doubt the possibility of an
autonomous African capitalism believe that these measures
have in fact made it even less likely. Indigenisation, they
argue, has in reality legitimised the operations of foreign
companies; certainly it was presented to foreign capitalists in
those terms and it only briefly checked continued foreign
investment in Nigeria. The critics also point out that in some
cases the transfer of ownership was fraudulent; in others it was
a transfer to employees or agents or distributors who could be
controlled by other means; and in the specific case of Kano,
Ankie Hoogvelt's penetrating research found that, up to 1978,
of the N15 million of shares divested to individuals other than
employees, no less than half had gone to only six of the city's
leading African businessmen, headed predictably by the
Dantata family – although it was significant that the shares did
go to businessmen and not, as in Zaire, to politicians. More
important, perhaps, transfer of ownership did not necessarily
mean transfer of control. Dr Hoogvelt found in Kano that the
large African shareholders created by indigenisation were more
active than she expected, but she also found that African
directors were not consulted on technological issues and that
many companies were tied to overseas partners by
technological agreements. She argued, in fact, that
indigenisation had shifted Nigeria into the phase of domination
through technology which, according to dependency theorists,
replaced more direct forms of domination in Latin America
after the Second World War.[87] Against this, however, it must
be added that the Nigerian government now insists that a
proportion of every company's executive directors must be
Africans and that management and technological agreements
must be subject to official scrutiny. There can be no doubt of
the sincere nationalism of the Nigerian Enterprises Promotions
Board or of their counterparts in the Kenyan Treasury.

Yet even if the radical critics were to be wrong and Kenyan and Nigerian enterprises managed to achieve substantial independence from foreign control, could they ever escape ultimate absorption by the state? This is the other side of radical scepticism about the possibility of African capitalism, best expressed in a splendid piece of polemic by a Nigerian socialist, O. F. Onoge. His central point is precisely that Nigeria is too late for capitalism: 'The Nigerian capitalist or aspirant, is a victim of historical developments. He is a late arrival on the historical stage.' His opportunity to exploit labour is limited, for unlike his European predecessors he cannot exploit workers in foreign countries, while even at home 'The Nigerian capitalist comes to play his part at a time when overtime pay, sick pay, casual leave, leave allowances and even pension fund have become part of his labourers' vocabulary. What is more, he comes at a time when capitalism itself as a social and cultural system, is being questioned.'[88] This is to put the problem of African capitalism into its proper context: the context of the internal class struggle within each African state, influenced by external pressures and events. But the weakness of Onoge's analysis is its implicit comparison with the early industrialisation of Britain and its neglect of the fact that late industrialisers like Japan have already carried through capitalist modernisations under the conditions he describes.

What then have emerged as the distinctive characteristics of African capitalism, in a global comparison? It was shaped first by the historical character of African societies. Their diversity when first brought into contact with the capitalist world economy led to diverse patterns of articulation and to a major contrast between West Africa on the one hand and eastern and southern Africa on the other. The prior existence of a capitalistic sector in West Africa enabled capitalism to develop more swiftly there and meant that its initial urban entrepreneurs came chiefly from trade and crafts, whereas in the east and south the entrepreneurs were chiefly products of the straddling process and sought to take over capitalist institutions created by immigrant businessmen. In both regions, however, underpopulation, the ample availability of land, the large measure of autonomy enjoyed by most small producers, the widespread experience of exchange, and the hedonistic pragmatism of African societies all combined to shape the character of capitalism. They explained both the weakness of resistance to its initial penetration, the frequent absorption of early rural capitalism into a synthesis with pre-capitalist elements, and the vigour with which these syntheses resisted the further evolution of capitalism. The same combination of circumstances also lay behind certain features of modern African industry, notably problems of management and work-discipline, and perhaps prevented labour relations in Africa from approximating to the Japanese model.

Yet not only were African societies distinctive, they were also exposed to a distinctive kind of capitalism: a very late capitalism, large in scale, sophisticated in technology, and already threatened by the rival force of socialism. In the early colonial period this foreign capitalism swamped a part of nineteenth-century Africa's commerce and shifted the continent's growth-points to agriculture. Only after 1945 did changes in international capitalism lead to a renewal of industrial growth within Africa. These new manufacturing industries were themselves products of late capitalism, creating major organisational problems for African entrepreneurs in dealing with modern technology, and breeding potential competition between alien and local manufacturers in which the state was the regulator. The central role of the African state, itself a contemporary of postwar industry, was perhaps the most important consequence of the lateness of African capitalism. It set a question-mark against the ability of even the most vigorous private enterprise to escape ultimate absorption into the public sector.

For the study of African capitalism must properly end with a question-mark. I have argued, as Colin Leys has argued, that capitalism does not necessarily either develop or underdevelop the countries of the periphery. Which it does in any individual country depends on the forces acting within that country, just as Robert Brenner suggested that responses to Malthusian crises in late medieval and early modern Europe varied with the structures of the different societies concerned.[89] Nigeria, Kenya, and a dozen other African states may move either towards national capitalism or away from it. They may make Africa a new bastion of capitalism in the world, just as it is already a bastion of Islam and Christianity. The issue is still wholly open. What is certain is that, as a result partly of prejudice and partly of socialist dogma, Africa's capitalists have not yet been taken seriously enough. And it is certain, too, that in determining whether or not African capitalism can establish itself as a creative force, political skill on both sides will be crucial, just as Roger Anstey showed that political skill was crucial to the abolition of the Atlantic slave trade.

CHAPTER 1: An Indigenous Capitalism?

1. Roger Anstey, *The Atlantic Slave Trade and British Abolition 1760–1810* (London: Macmillan, 1975). For comment, see Christine Bolt and Seymour Drescher (eds), *Anti-Slavery, Religion, and Reform: Essays in Memory of Roger Anstey* (Folkestone: Dawson, 1980).
2. See esp. Roger Anstey, *Britain and the Congo in the Nineteenth Century* (Oxford: Clarendon, 1962) and *King Leopold's Legacy: the Congo under Belgian Rule 1908–1960* (London: Oxford University Press, 1966).
3. Karl Marx, 'The British Rule in India', in *Karl Marx and Friedrich Engels, Selected Works* 2 vols (Moscow: Foreign Languages Publishing House, 1958) vol. I, p. 351.
4. Karl Marx, *Capital*, English translation, 3 vols (Moscow: Foreign Languages Publishing House, 1966) vol. III, pp. 333–4.
5. Colin Leys, 'Kenya: What Does "Dependency" Explain?', *Review of African Political Economy*, XVII (January 1980) 109.
6. Julius Nyerere, 'The Rational Choice' (1973), in Andrew Coulson (ed.), *African Socialism in Practice: the Tanzanian Experience* (Nottingham: Spokesman, 1979) pp.19–26.
7. Rhoda Howard, *Colonialism and Underdevelopment in Ghana* (London: Croom Helm, 1978); Mahmood Mamdani, *Politics and Class Formation in Uganda* (New York: Monthly Review, 1976); Gavin Kitching, *Class and Economic Change in Kenya: the Making of an African Petite Bourgeoisie 1905–1970* (New Haven: Yale University Press, 1980).
8. Nicola Swainson, *The Development of Corporate Capitalism in Kenya 1918–77* (London: William Heinemann, 1980); Apollo L. Njonjo, 'The Africanisation of the "White Highlands": a Study in Agrarian Class Struggles in Kenya, 1950–1974', Ph.D. thesis, Princeton University, 1977.
9. *African Business* (May 1979) 73.
10. Swainson, *Development*, pp. 204–6, 270–3; *The Weekly Review* (7 August 1981) 28; Rafael Kaplinsky, 'Capitalist Accumulation in the Periphery – the Kenyan Case Re-examined', *Review of African Political Economy*, XVII (January 1980) 90–9.
11. M.-C. Diop, 'Les Affaires mourides à Dakar', *Politique africaine*, I, 4 (Novembre 1981) 97.
12. J. H. Price, 'Alhaji Alhassan Dantata – an appreciation', *West Africa* (29 October 1955) 1,020.

13. *The Weekly Review* (15 May 1981) 11–13.
14. Marx, *Capital*, vol. III, p. 880.
15. V. I. Lenin, 'The Development of Capitalism in Russia' (1899), in his *Collected Works*, English translation (Moscow: Progress Publishers, 1964) vol. III, pp. 21–607; Maurice Dobb, *Studies in the Development of Capitalism* (London: Routledge and Kegan Paul, 1946).
16. Max Weber, *The Protestant Ethic and the Spirit of Capitalism*, trans. T. Parsons, 2nd edn (London: George Allen & Unwin, 1976) pp. 13–31.
17. Maxime Rodinson, *Islam and Capitalism*, trans. B. Pearce (London: Allen Lane, 1974) p.184.
18. Ibid., p. 7.
19. Dixon Denham and Hugh Clapperton, *Narrative of Travels and Discoveries in Northern and Central Africa* (London: John Murray, 1826) part 2, p. 40.
20. André Salifou, 'Malan Yaroh, un grand négociant du Soudan central à la fin du XIXe siècle', *Journal de la Société des Africanistes*, XLII (1972) 12.
21. Timothy F. Garrard, *Akan Weights and the Gold Trade* (London: Longman, 1980) pp. 6–15; Marion Johnson, 'The Cowrie Currencies of West Africa, part I', *Journal of African History*, XI (1970) 18; Lars Sundström, *The Exchange Economy of Pre-Colonial Tropical Africa* (reprinted, London: Hurst, 1974) pp. 34–6.
22. Denham and Clapperton, *Narrative*, part 2, p. 44.
23. Stephen Baier, *An Economic History of Central Niger* (Oxford: Clarendon, 1980) p. 69.
24. Marx, *Capital*, vol. II (1961) p. 34, and vol. III, pp. 325–35.
25. René Caillié, *Travels Through Central Africa to Timbuctoo*, English translation, 2 vols (reprinted, London: Frank Cass, 1968) vol. I, pp. 340–1, 354. The Bambara were the local non-Muslim people.
26. Charles Monteil, *Monographie de Djénné: cercle et ville* (Tulle: Mazéyrie, 1903) p. 164; Mary Tiffen, *The Enterprising Peasant: Economic Development in Gombe Emirate, 1900–1968* (London: HMSO, 1976) pp. 112–13.
27. M. I. Finley, *The Ancient Economy* (reprinted, London: Chatto & Windus, 1975) p. 66.
28. Philip D. Curtin, *Economic Change in Precolonial Africa: Senegambia in the Era of the Slave Trade* (Madison: University of Wisconsin Press, 1975) p. 286 n. 8.
29. Yves Person, *Samori: une révolution dyula*, 3 vols (Dakar: Institut Fondamental d'Afrique Noire, 1968–75) vol. I, p. 114; Emmanuel Terray, 'La Captivité dans le royaume abron du Gyaman', in Claude Meillassoux (ed.), *L'Esclavage en Afrique précoloniale* (Paris: Maspero, 1975) p. 428; A. Mischlich, *Ueber die Kulturen im Mittel-Sudan* (Berlin: Reimer, 1942) pp. 87, 73.
30. 'Deji Ogunremi, 'Human Porterage in Nigeria in the Nineteenth Century', *Journal of the Historical Society of Nigeria*, VIII, 1 (December 1975) 37–45.
31. For these points, see Finley, *Ancient Economy*, pp. 65–73.

32. Richard Roberts, 'Long Distance Trade and Production: Sinsani in the Nineteenth Century', *Journal of African History*, XXI (1980) 175; Sundström, *Exchange Economy*, p. 147; Éric Pollet and Grace Winter, *La Société soninké (Dyahunu, Mali)* (Bruxelles: Institut de Sociologie, Université Libre de Bruxelles, 1971) p. 244.

33. Monteil, *Monographie*, pp. 175–215. A slightly revised version later appeared: Charles Monteil, *Une Cité soudanaise: Djénné, métropole du delta central du Niger* (Paris: Société d'Editions Géographiques, Maritimes et Coloniales, 1932).

34. Monteil, *Monographie*, p. 208.

35. Mischlich, *Kulturen*. For an English version, see Douglas E. Ferguson, 'Nineteenth Century Hausaland, Being a Description by Imam Imoru of the Land, Economy, and Society of his People', Ph.D. thesis, University of California at Los Angeles, 1973.

36. C. H. Robinson, *Hausaland* (new edn, London: Samson Low, Marston, 1897) p. 113; Marion Johnson, 'Technology, Competition, and African Crafts', in Clive Dewey and A. G. Hopkins (eds), *The Imperial Impact* (London: Athlone Press, 1978) p. 265.

37. Heinrich Barth, *Travels and Discoveries in North and Central Africa*, English translation, reprinted, 3 vols (London: Frank Cass, 1965) vol. I, p. 512.

38. See Paul E. Lovejoy, 'Interregional Monetary Flows in the Precolonial Trade of Nigeria', *Journal of African History*, XV (1974) 563–85.

39. Jacques Meniaud, *Haut-Sénégal-Niger (Soudan Français): géographie économique*, 2 vols (Paris: Lerose, 1912) vol. II, p. 221.

40. Mischlich, *Kulturen*, p. 47.

41. Philip J. Shea, 'Economies of Scale and the Indigo Dyeing Industry of Precolonial Kano', *Kano Studies,* new series, I (1974/7) 55–61, and 'The Development of an Export Oriented Dyed Cloth Industry in Kano Emirate in the Nineteenth Century', Ph.D. thesis, University of Wisconsin, 1975.

42. See esp. Baier, *Economic History*, pp. 27, 48, 51, 54, 69. There is important material on this subject in Yusufu Bala Usman, 'The Transformation of Katsina, *c.*1796–1903' (Ph.D. thesis, Ahmadu Bello University, Zaria, 1974) and Ibrahim A. Tahir, 'Scholars, Sufis, Saints and Capitalists in Kano, 1904–1974' (Ph.D. thesis, Cambridge University, 1975).

43. Salifou, 'Malan Yaroh', p. 11.

44. [L. G.] Binger, *Du Niger au Golfe de Guinée*, 2 vols (Paris: Hachette, 1892) vol. II, p. 50.

45. Kang Chao, *The Development of Cotton Textile Production in China* (Cambridge, Mass: Harvard University East Asian Research Center, 1977) pp. 30–4.

46. Paul E. Lovejoy, 'The Characteristics of Plantations in the Nineteenth-Century Sokoto Caliphate', *American Historical Review*, LXXXIV (1979) 1,291.

47. Joseph Needham, 'Science and Society in East and West', in his *The Grand Titration* (reprinted, London: George Allen & Unwin, 1979) pp. 190–217; Immanuel Wallerstein, *The Modern World System*, vol. I (New York: Academic Press, 1974) p. 52.

48. M. G. Smith, *The Economy of Hausa Communities of Zaria* (London: HMSO, 1955) pp. 92, 101; Murray Last, *The Sokoto Caliphate* (reprinted, London: Longman, 1977) p. 106; Robinson, *Hausaland*, p. 204.

49. Baier, *Economic History*, ch. 8; Paul E. Lovejoy, 'The Hausa Kola Trade (1700–1900)', Ph.D. thesis, University of Wisconsin, 1973, p. 220.

50. Clifford Geertz, *Peddlers and Princes: Social Change and Economic Modernization in Two Indonesian Towns* (Chicago: University of Chicago, 1963) pp. 28–9.

51. De Marees, quoted in J. D. Fage, 'Slaves and Society in Western Africa, *c.*1445–*c.*1700', *Journal of African History*, XXI (1980) 305.

52. Magnus J. Sampson, *Gold Coast Men of Affairs* (reprinted, London: Dawson, 1969) p. 101.

53. Andrew Swanzy, 'Civilisation and Progress on the Gold Coast of Africa', *Journal of the Society of Arts*, XXIII (1874–5) 422–3; Edward Reynolds, *Trade and Economic Change on the Gold Coast, 1807–1874* (Harlow: Longman, 1974) p. 106.

54. Kwame Y. Daaku, 'Trade and Trading Patterns of the Akan in the Seventeenth and Eighteenth Centuries', in Claude Meillassoux (ed.), *The Development of Indigenous Trade and Markets in West Africa* (London: Oxford University Press, 1971) p. 174. See also R. A. Kea, 'The "Laboring Classes" in 17th and 18th Century Gold Coast States', African Studies Association of the United States Conference Paper, Philadelphia, October 1980.

55. This section is based chiefly on Ivor Wilks, *Asante in the Nineteenth Century* (Cambridge: Cambridge University Press, 1975) and 'The Golden Stool and the Elephant Tail: an Essay on Wealth in Asante', *Research in Economic Anthropology*, II (1979) 1–36.

56. Quoted in Kwame Arhin, 'Some Asante Views of Colonial Rule: as Seen in the Controversy Relating to Death Duties', *Transactions of the Historical Society of Ghana*, XV, 1 (June 1974) 76.

57. Kwame Arhin, 'Aspects of the Ashanti Northern Trade in the Nineteenth Century', *Africa*, XL (1970) 366.

58. R. S. Rattray, *Religion and Art in Ashanti* (Oxford: Clarendon, 1927) chs 23–8; Marion Johnson, 'Ashanti Craft Organization', *African Arts*, XIII, 1 (November 1979) 60–3, 78–82.

59. Ivor Wilks, 'Land, Labour, Capital and the Forest Kingdom of Asante', in J. Friedman and M. J. Rowlands (eds), *The Evolution of Social Systems* (Pittsburgh: University of Pittsburgh, 1978) pp. 487–8, 500–1. See also T. C. McCaskie, 'Office, Land and Subjects in the History of the Manwere Fekuo of Kumase', *Journal of African History*, XXI (1980) 192, 195.

60. Hermann Pössinger, 'Interrelations Between Economic and Social Change in Rural Africa: the Case of the Ovimbundu of Angola', in Franz-Wilhelm Heimer (ed.), *Social Change in Angola* (München: Weltforum Verlag, 1973) p. 37.

61. David Birmingham, 'The Coffee Barons of Cazengo', *Journal of African History*, XIX (1978) 528–9.

62.   Robert J. Cummings, 'The Early Development of Akamba Local Trade History, *c.*1780–1820', *Kenya Historical Review*, IV, 1 (1976) 85–110.

63.   John Iliffe, *A Modern History of Tanganyika* (Cambridge: Cambridge University Press, 1979) p. 46; C. S. Nicholls, *The Swahili Coast* (London: George Allen & Unwin, 1971) p. 293; Richard F. Burton, *The Lake Regions of Central Africa* (reprinted, 2 vols, New York: Horizon Press, 1961) vol. I, p. 18.

64.   E.g. Gerald W. Hartwig, *The Art of Survival in East Africa: the Kerebe and Long-Distance Trade, 1800–1895* (New York: Africana Publishing Company, 1976) p. 53.

65.   P. Cowen, 'Differentiation in a Kenya Location', East African Universities Social Science Conference Paper, Nairobi, 1972, pp. 3–4.

66.   Richard Pankhurst, *Economic History of Ethiopia 1800–1935* (Addis Ababa: Haile Sellassie University Press, 1968) pp. 46–7.

67.   *Church Missionary Intelligencer*, VII (1882) 726.

68.   Mackay to Kirk, 8 June 1885, Public Record Office, London, Foreign Office 84/1727/146.

69.   François Coillard, *On the Threshold of Central Africa* (3rd edn, London: Frank Cass, 1971) p. 362.

70.   Colin Bundy, *The Rise and Fall of the South African Peasantry* (London: Heinemann, 1979) p. 94

71.   Norman Etherington, *Preachers, Peasants and Politics in Southeast Africa, 1835–1880* (London: Royal Historical Society, 1978).

72.   Bundy, *Rise and Fall*, p. 93.

73.   Quoted in ibid.

74.   Robert Campbell, *A Pilgrimage to My Motherland* (London: Johnson, [1861?]) pp. 57–8.

75.   Quoted in Claude-Hélène Perrot, 'Or, richesse et pouvoir chez les Anyi-Ndenye aux XVIIIe et XIXe siècles', *Journal des Africanistes*, XLVIII (1978) 101.

76.   E. E. Evans-Pritchard, *Nuer Religion* (reprinted, New York: Oxford University Press, 1977) p. 154. For pragmatism, see Louis-Vincent Thomas, *Les Diola*, 2 vols (Dakar: Institut Fondamental d'Afrique Noire, 1959) vol. II, pp. 634, 791–5. For the identification of material prosperity with spiritual force, see Marc Augé, *Théorie des pouvoirs et idéologie: étude de cas en Côte d'Ivoire* (Paris: Hermann, 1975) passim.

77.   Quoted in Abba Ashigar, 'Mallamti Settlements: Some Aspects of Their Role in the History of Borno', B.A. thesis, Abdullahi Bayero College, Kano, 1977, p. 39.

78.   Paul Riesman, *Freedom in Fulani Social Life*, trans. M. Fuller (Chicago: University of Chicago, 1977) pp. 139, 231; Sinali Coulibaly, *Le Paysan sénoufo* (Abidjan: Nouvelles Editions Africaines, 1978) p. 101.

79.   T. E. Bowdich, *Mission from Cape Coast Castle to Ashantee* (3rd edn, London: Frank Cass, 1966) p. 292.

80.   Richard N. Henderson. *The King in Every Man: Evolutionary Trends in Onitsha Ibo Society and Culture* (New Haven: Yale University Press, 1972) p. 260.

81.   Wole Soyinka, *Death and the King's Horseman* (London: Eyre Methuen, 1975) p. 14.

82. Weber, *Protestant Ethic*, p. 95.
83. W. J. Argyle, *The Fon of Dahomey* (Oxford: Clarendon, 1966) p. 97.

CHAPTER 2: Capitalists and Peasants

1   Marion Johnson, 'Technology, Competition and African Crafts', in Clive Dewey and A. G. Hopkins (eds), *The Imperial Impact* (London: Athlone Press, 1978) pp. 259–69.
2.   Samir Amin, *Le Monde des affaires sénégalais* (Paris: Editions de Minuit, 1969) pp. 11–29; André Salifou, 'Malan Yaroh, un grand négociant du Soudan central à la fin du XIXe siècle', *Journal de la Société des Africanistes*, XLII (1972) 22–6; Stephen Baier, *An Economic History of Central Niger* (Oxford: Clarendon, 1980) p. 100.
3.   Fred I. A. Omu, *Press and Politics in Nigeria, 1880–1937* (London: Longman, 1978) p. 105. For trade in Lagos, see Antony G. Hopkins, 'An Economic History of Lagos, 1880–1914', Ph.D. thesis, University of London, 1964.
4.   Jan S. Hogendorn, *Nigerian Groundnut Exports: Origins and Early Development* (Zaria: Ahmadu Bello University Press, 1978).
5.   Frederick Cooper, 'Africa and the World Economy', African Studies Association of the United States Conference Paper, Bloomington, October 1981, p. 37.
6.   Polly Hill, *The Gold Coast Cocoa Farmer* (London: Oxford University Press, 1956) and *The Migrant Cocoa-Farmers of Southern Ghana* (Cambridge: Cambridge University Press, 1963).
7.   R. Szereszewski, *Structural Changes in the Economy of Ghana 1891–1911* (London: Weidenfeld and Nicolson, 1965) pp. 53, 1.
8.   Ivor Wilks, 'Land, Labour, Capital and the Forest Kingdom of Asante', in J. Friedman and M. J. Rowlands (eds), *The Evolution of Social Systems* (Pittsburgh: University of Pittsburgh Press, 1978) p. 501; Andrew A. Opoku, 'Across the Prah', in Hill, *Migrant*, p. 30.
9.   The following account draws largely on A. F. Robertson, 'Abusa: the Structural History of an Economic Contract', *Journal of Development Studies*, forthcoming.
10. Hill, *Migrant*, pp. 17, 187; Szereszewski, *Structural*, pp. 55–8.
11. Hill, *Gold Coast*, pp. 25–6, 35; W. H. Beckett, *Koransang 1904–1970* (Institute of Statistical, Social and Economic Research, Legon: Technical Publications Series No. 31, 1972) p. 18.
12. W. H. Beckett, *Akokoaso: a Survey of a Gold Coast Village* (London School of Economics Monographs on Social Anthropology No. 10, 1944) esp. p. 87.
13. W. H. Beckett, *Koransang: a Gold Coast Cocoa Farm* (Accra: Government Printer, 1945) pp. 11–12; Beckett, *Koransang 1904–1970*, part 2.
14. Hill, *Gold Coast*, pp. 8–9.
15. See esp. Philippe Lena, 'Le Problème de la main-d'oeuvre en zone pionnière, quelques points de repère', *Cahiers du CIRES*, XXIII (Décembre 1979) 89–98.
16. H. Lefebvre, quoted in A. F. Robertson, 'On Sharecropping', *Man*, NS, XV (1980) 412.

17. See Jean Tricart, 'Le Café en Côte d'Ivoire', *Cahiers d'outre-mer*, X (1957) 219; Gabriel Rougerie, 'Les Pays agni du sud-est de la Côte d'Ivoire forestière: essai de géographie humaine', *Etudes éburnéennes*, VI (1957) 111–13; M. Dupire, 'Planteurs autochtones et étrangers en Basse-Côte d'Ivoire orientale', ibid., VIII (1960) 29–39; David H. Groff, 'The Development of Capitalism in the Ivory Coast: the Case of Assikasso, 1880–1940', Ph.D. thesis, Stanford University, 1980, pp. 364–8; Jean-Pierre Chauveau and Jacques Richard, 'Une "Périphérie recentrée": à propos d'un système local d'économie de plantation en Côte d'Ivoire', *Cahiers d'études africaines*, XVII (1977) 491–3, 513; Lena, 'Le Problème', p. 93.
18. Robertson, 'Abusa'.
19. C. Okali and R. A. Kotey, *Akokoaso: a Resurvey* (Institute of Statistical, Social and Economic Research, Legon: Technical Publication Series No. 15, 1971) pp. 14–17.
20. Björn Beckman, *Organising the Farmers: Cocoa Politics and National Development in Ghana* (Uppsala: Scandinavian Institute of African Studies, 1976) pp. 36, 279; *West Africa* (29 June 1981) p. 1,484.
21. Björn Beckman, 'Ghana, 1951–78: the Agrarian Basis of the Post-Colonial State', in Judith Heyer and others (eds), *Rural Development in Tropical Africa* (London: Macmillan, 1981) p. 164.
22. *West Africa* (22 March 1982) p. 785.
23. Tom W. Shick, *Behold the Promised Land: a History of Afro-American Settler Society in Nineteenth-Century Liberia* (Baltimore: Johns Hopkins University Press, 1977) pp. 112–16.
24. J. B. Webster, 'Agege: Plantations and the African Church, 1901–20', in Nigerian Institute of Social and Economic Research, *Conference Proceedings, March 1962* (n.p., 1963) pp. 124–30; A. G. Hopkins, 'Innovation in a Colonial Context: African Origins of the Nigerian Cocoa-Farming Industry, 1880–1920', in Dewey and Hopkins, *Imperial Impact*, pp. 83–96.
25. J. D. Hargreaves, *A Life of Sir Samuel Lewis* (London: Oxford University Press, 1958) pp. 27–8, 62.
26. Kwame Arhin, *West African Traders in Ghana in the Nineteenth and Twentieth Centuries* (London: Longman, 1979) p. 15.
27. A. W. Cardinall, *In Ashanti and Beyond* (London: Seeley Service, 1927) p.99.
28. From my notes of a seminar at Cambridge, 25 February 1981. See also J. C. Muir, 'Survey of Cacao Areas – Western Province, Ashanti', Department of Agriculture, Gold Coast, Bulletin No. 22 (1930) 61.
29. Walker to Cyril Walker, 19 October 1894, Walker Papers (Accession 88), Church Missionary Society Archives, Birmingham University Library.
30. *Church Missionary Intelligencer*, XX (1895) 681.
31. See, e.g., O. F. Raum, 'German East Africa: Changes in African Life under German Administration, 1892–1914', in Vincent Harlow and E. M. Chilver (eds), *History of East Africa*, vol. II (Oxford: Clarendon, 1965) p.193; Chantal Savignac, 'Approche des conditions de travail en agriculture dans le nord de la Côte-d'Ivoire', *Cahiers du CIRES*, XXII (Septembre 1979) 34.

32. Walker to his father, 12 December 1898, Walker Papers (above, n. 29).

33. *Church Missionary Intelligencer*, XXV (1900) 341.

34. C. C. Wrigley, 'The Changing Economic Structure of Buganda', in L. A. Fallers (ed.), *The King's Men* (London: Oxford University Press, 1964) p. 34.

35. R. A. Snoxall (ed.), *Luganda-English Dictionary* (Oxford: Clarendon, 1967) s.v. kusenga, kwesengerera.

36. M. P. Cowen, 'Differentiation in a Kenya Location', East African Universities Social Science Conference Paper, Nairobi, 1972, pp. 6–17.

37. Edgar Bowden and Jon Moris, 'Social Characteristics of Progressive Baganda Farmers', *East African Journal of Rural Development*, II (1969) 56, 61.

38. Tshilemalema Mukenge, 'Les Hommes d'affaires zairois: du travail salarié à l'entreprise personnelle', *Canadian Journal of African Studies*, VII (1973) 455–75.

39. Maud S. Muntemba, 'Regional and Social Differentiation in Broken Hill Rural District, Northern Rhodesia, 1930–1964', in Martin A. Klein (ed.), *Peasants in Africa* (Beverly Hills: Sage, 1980) pp. 263–4.

40. A. K. H. Weinrich, *African Farmers in Rhodesia* (London: Oxford University Press, 1975) chs 6 and 11.

41. Gavin Kitching, *Class and Economic Change in Kenya: the Making of an African Petite Bourgeoisie 1905–1970* (New Haven: Yale University Press, 1980) ch. 8.

42. Hill, *Migrant*, pp. 168–9.

43. Roger Walke, 'Report on a Study of Private Rubber Farmers', *Liberian Research Association Journal*, III (1971) 44.

44. Samir Amin, *Le Développement du capitalisme en Côte d'Ivoire* (Paris: Editions de Minuit, 1967) p. 101.

45. Pierre-Philippe Rey, *Colonialisme, néo-colonialisme et transition au capitalisme: exemple de la 'Comilog' au Congo-Brazzaville* (Paris: Maspero, 1971) p. 365.

46. Idem, *Les Alliances de classes* (Paris: Maspero, 1973) passim.

47. Aiden Foster-Carter, 'Can we Articulate "Articulation"?' in John Clammer (ed.), *The New Economic Anthropology* (London: Macmillan, 1978) p. 243.

48. J. D. Y. Peel, 'Inequality and Action: the Forms of Ijesha Social Conflict', *Canadian Journal of African Studies*, XIV (1980) 483; Jeanne K. Henn, 'Peasants, Workers, and Capital: the Political Economy of Labor and Incomes in Cameroon', Ph.D. thesis, Harvard University, 1978, pp. 134–5, 263.

49. Peter Geschiere, 'The Articulation of Different Modes of Production: Old and New Inequalities in Maka Villages (Southeast Cameroon)', *African Perspectives* (1978/2) 45–68.

50. Rey, *Les Alliances*, pp. 215–16.

51. Karl Marx, 'Oekonomische Manuskripte 1857/58', in Karl Marx and Friedrich Engels, *Gesamtausgabe*, section 2, vol. 1, part 1 (Berlin: Dietz, 1976) p. 33.

52.   For the recent history of the cocoa industry, see Beckman, *Organising the Farmers*.

53.   Here I disagree with Kitching, *Class,* ch. 14.

54.   Polly Hill, *Rural Hausa: a Village and a Setting* (Cambridge: Cambridge University Press, 1972) p. 188; J. Weber, 'La Région cacaoyère du centre sud Cameroun', in Samir Amin (ed.), *L'Agriculture africaine et le capitalisme* (Paris: Anthropos, 1975) pp. 91–105; Gilles Sautter, *De l'Atlantique au fleuve Congo: une géographie du sous-peuplement*, 2 vols (Paris: Mouton, 1966) vol. II, p. 934.

55.   Leroy Vail and Landeg White, *Capitalism and Colonialism in Mozambique* (London: Heinemann, 1980) passim, esp. p. 3.

56.   See Frederick Cooper, *From Slaves to Squatters: Plantation Labor and Agriculture in Zanzibar and Coastal Kenya, 1890–1925* (New Haven: Yale University Press, 1980); A. M. H. Sheriff, 'The Zanzibari Peasantry under Imperialism 1873–1964', *Maji Maji* (Dar es Salaam), XXVIII (November 1976) 1–34.

57.   Roger J. Southall, 'Farmers, Traders and Brokers in the Gold Coast Economy', *Canadian Journal of African Studies*, XII (1978) 206–9.

58.   See Tony Barnett, *The Gezira Scheme: an Illusion of Development* (London: Frank Cass, 1977); Mark R. Duffield, *Maiurno: Capitalism and Rural Life in Sudan* (London: Ithaca Press, 1981).

59.   C. C. F. Dundas, 'Native Coffee Cultivation on Kilimanjaro', 12 May 1924, Public Record Office, London, Colonial Office 691/70/379.

60.   John Iliffe, *A Modern History of Tanganyika* (Cambridge: Cambridge University Press, 1979) pp. 274–86.

61.   Henn, 'Peasants', p. 313.

62.   A. Mafeje, *Agrarian Revolution and the Land Question in Buganda* (Institute of Social Studies, The Hague: Occasional Paper No. 32, 1973) pp. 8–15; Henry W. West, *Land Policy in Buganda* (Cambridge: Cambridge University Press, 1972) pp. 19, 116.

63.   L. P. Mair, *An African People in the Twentieth Century* (London: Routledge, 1934) pp. 123, 128.

64.   Quoted in Audrey I. Richards (ed.), *Economic Development and Tribal Change* (revised edition, Nairobi: Oxford University Press, 1973) p. 127.

65.   Audrey I. Richards, *The Changing Structure of a Ganda Village* (Nairobi: East African Publishing House, 1966) p. 24.

66.   Mair, *African People*, pp. 152–3.

67.   Mafeje, *Agrarian Revolution*, pp. 19–20; A. F. Robertson and G. A. Hughes, 'The Family Farm in Buganda', *Development and Change*, IX (1978) 415–37.

68.   R. Galletti and others, *Nigerian Cocoa Farmers* (London: Oxford University Press, 1956). The point is made even more clearly by Sara S. Berry, 'Export Growth, Entrepreneurship and Class Formation in Rural Western Nigeria', in Raymond E. Dumett and Lawrence J. Brainard (eds), *Problems of Rural Development* (Leiden: Brill, 1975) esp. p. 91.

69.   Michael Cowen, 'Commodity Production in Kenya's Central Province', in Heyer, *Rural Development*, pp. 121–42.

70. Apollo L. Njonjo, 'The Africanisation of the "White Highlands": a Study in Agrarian Class Struggles in Kenya, 1950–1974', Ph.D. thesis, Princeton University, 1977.

71. Ibid., p. 28.

72. Arthur Hazlewood, *The Economy of Kenya: the Kenyatta Era* (Oxford: Oxford University Press, 1979) p. 35.

73. Colin Leys, 'Capital Accumulation, Class Formation and Dependency – the Significance of the Kenyan Case', *Socialist Register* (1978) p. 254.

74. David Brokensha and Bernard Riley, 'Vegetation Changes in Mbere Division, Embu', and David Brokensha and E. H. N. Njeru, 'Some Consequences of Land Adjudication in Mbere Division, Embu', Institute of Development Studies, Nairobi, Working Papers Nos 319 and 320, September 1977.

75. Colin Leys, 'Development Strategy in Kenya Since 1971', *Canadian Journal of African Studies*, XIII (1979) 302–3, 317–20; Njonjo, 'Africanisation', pp. 504–17.

76. Neil Parsons, 'The Economic History of Khama's Country in Botswana, 1844–1930', in Robin Palmer and Neil Parsons (eds), *The Roots of Rural Poverty in Central and Southern Africa* (London: Heinemann, 1977) p. 119.

77. See Christopher Colclough and Stephen McCarthy, *The Political Economy of Botswana: a Study of Growth and Distribution* (Oxford: Oxford University Press, 1980) passim.

78. Isobel Winter, 'The Post-Colonial State and the Forces and Relations of Production: Swaziland', *Review of African Political Economy*, IX (May 1978) 27–43; Carolyn L. Baylies, 'Class Formation and the State in Zambia', Ph.D. thesis, University of Wisconsin, 1978, pp. 754–90.

79. Weinrich, *African Farmers*, ch. 7; Barry Munslow, 'Zimbabwe's Emerging African Bourgeoisie', *Review of African Political Economy*, XIX (September 1980) 65–7.

80. *The Weekly Review*, 4 September 1981, p. 15.

CHAPTER 3: Capitalists and Preachers

1. Hope Masterton Waddell, *Twenty-Nine Years in the West Indies and Central Africa, 1829–1858* (2nd edn, London: Frank Cass, 1970) p. 377.

2. See Daryll Forde (ed.), *Efik Traders of Old Calabar* (London: Oxford University Press, 1956); A. J. H. Latham, *Old Calabar 1600–1891* (Oxford: Oxford University Press, 1973).

3. Robin Horton, 'Destiny and the Unconscious in West Africa', *Africa*, XXXI (1961) 114.

4. Jan Vansina, *The Children of Woot: a History of the Kuba Peoples* (Madison: University of Wisconsin Press, 1978) p. 184.

5. Norman Long, *Social · Change and the Individual* (Manchester: Manchester University Press, 1968). For related findings, see Karla O. Poewe, 'Matriliny and Capitalism: the Development of Incipient Classes in Luapula, Zambia', *Dialectical Anthropology*, III (1978) 331–47.

6.   Above, chapter 2, n. 24.
7.   Colette Piault (ed.), *Prophétisme et thérapeutique: Albert Atcho et la communauté de Bregbo* (Paris: Hermann, 1975).
8.   Ibid., p. 106.
9.   Ibid., pp. 56–9.
10. Marc Augé, 'Les Faiseurs d'ombre: servitude et structure lignagère dans la société alladian', in Claude Meillassoux (ed.), *L'Esclavage en Afrique précoloniale* (Paris: Maspero, 1975) p. 465 n. 5.
11. Sheila S. Walker, 'Young Men, Old Men, and Devils in Aeroplanes: the Harrist Church, the Witchcraft Complex and Social Change in the Ivory Coast', *Journal of Religion in Africa*, XI (1980) 116.
12. András Zempléni, 'De la Persécution à la culpabilité', in Piault, *Prophétisme*, p. 156.
13. See Christopher Hill, *Society and Puritanism in Pre-Revolutionary England* (London: Secker & Warburg, 1964).
14. David J. Parkin, *Palms, Wine, and Witnesses: Public Spirit and Private Gain in an African Farming Community* (London: Intertext, 1972).
15. Stephen Baier, *An Economic History of Central Niger* (Oxford: Clarendon, 1980) pp. 65–7.
16. John N. Paden, *Religion and Political Culture in Kano* (Berkeley: University of California, 1973) chs 2 and 3.
17. Abner Cohen, *Custom and Politics in Urban Africa: a Study of Hausa Migrants in Yoruba Towns* (London: Routledge & Kegan Paul, 1969) pp. 141–60.
18. Lansiné Kaba, *The Wahhabiyya: Islamic Reform and Politics in French West Africa* (Evanston: North-western University Press, 1974) passim.
19. See John P. Halstead, 'A Comparative Historical Study of Colonial Nationalism in Egypt and Morocco', *African Historical Studies*, II (1969) 92–3; Raymond Delval, 'Les Musulmans d'Abidjan', *Cahiers du CHEAM*, No. 10 (Paris, 1980) pp. 51–9.
20. Jean-Loup Amselle, *Les Négociants de la savane: histoire et organisation sociale des Kooroko (Mali)* (Paris: Anthropos, 1977) pp. 245–59.
21. Jean Copans, *Les Marabouts de l'arachide: la confrérie mouride et les paysans du Sénégal* (Paris: Sycomore, 1980) pp. 222–7; Donal B. Cruise O'Brien, *The Mourides of Senegal* (Oxford: Clarendon, 1971) p. 3; M.C. Diop, 'Les Affaires mourides à Dakar', *Politique africaine*, I, 4 (Novembre 1981) 90–100.
22. See E. A. Ayandele, *The Missionary Impact on Modern Nigeria* (reprinted, London: Longman, 1977) pp. 267–78; Richard L. Sklar, *Nigerian Political Parties* (Princeton: Princeton University Press, 1963) pp. 253–4.
23. Stephen S. Hlophe, *Class, Ethnicity and Politics in Liberia* (Washington, D.C.: University Press of America, 1979) p. 187; Abner Cohen, 'The Politics of Ritual Secrecy', *Man*, NS, VI (1971) 427–48.
24. M. J. Field, *Search for Security: an Ethno-Psychiatric Study of Rural Ghana* (London: Faber, 1960) p. 87.
25. Ibid., pp. 105, 108.
26. Ibid., p. 112.

27. Lloyd W. Swantz, 'The Role of the Medicine Man among the Zaramo of Dar es Salaam', Ph.D. thesis, University of Dar es Salaam, 1974, p. 81.

28. Michael Taussig, 'The Genesis of Capitalism Amongst a South American Peasantry: Devil's Labour and the Baptism of Money', *Comparative Studies in Society and History*, XIX (1977) 130–55.

29. Robert W. Harms, *River of Wealth, River of Sorrow: the Central Zaire Basin in the Era of the Slave and Ivory Trade, 1500–1891* (New Haven: Yale University Press, 1981) pp. 197–201.

30. Monica Wilson, *Communal Rituals of the Nyakyusa* (London: Oxford University Press, 1959) p. 59; A. K. H. Weinrich, *Black and White Elites in Rural Rhodesia* (Manchester University Press, 1973) p. 202; R. E. S. Tanner, 'The Sorcerer in Northern Sukumaland', *South-western Journal of Anthropology*, XII (1966) 439.

31. Alan Macfarlane, *The Origins of English Individualism* (Oxford: Basil Blackwood, 1978) p. 2; Keith Thomas, 'The Relevance of Social Anthropology to the Historical Study of English Witchcraft', in Mary Douglas (ed.), *Witchcraft Confessions and Accusations* (London: Tavistock, 1970) pp. 62–3.

32. P. M. van Hekken and H. U. E. Thoden van Velzen, *Land Scarcity and Rural Inequality in Tanzania* (The Hague: Mouton, 1972) pp. 60–1.

33. N. O. Addo, 'Attitudes and Opinions of Cocoa Farmers to Matters Related to Work and Employment', *Ghana Journal of Sociology*, VII, 2 (January 1974) 39.

34. G. Ancey, J. Chevassu and J. Michotte, *L'Economie de l'espace rural de la région de Bouaké* (Paris: O.R.S.T.O.M., 1974) p. 23.

35. Terence J. Johnson, 'Protest: Tradition and Change: an Analysis of Southern Gold Coast Riots 1890–1920', *Economy and Society*, I (1972) 179.

36. *Tanganyika Times* (Dar es Salaam), 12 January 1929. 221996

37. D. A. Low, 'The Advent of Populism in Buganda', *Comparative Studies in Society and History*, VI (1963–4) 424–44; J. M. Fortt, 'Land Tenure and the Emergence of Large Scale Farming', in Audrey I. Richards, Ford Sturrock and Jean M. Fortt (eds), *Subsistence to Commercial Farming in Present-Day Buganda* (Cambridge: Cambridge University Press, 1973) p. 76.

38. Steven Feierman, 'Change in African Therapeutic Systems', *Social Science and Medicine*, XIIIB (1979) 277–8; Una Maclean, 'Some Aspects of Sickness Behaviour Among the Yoruba', in J. B. Loudon (ed.), *Social Anthropology and Medicine* (London: Academic Press, 1976) pp. 314–15.

39. See Paul Pélissier, *Les paysans du Sénégal* (Saint-Yrieix: Fabrègue, 1966) p. 736.

40. Nehemiah Levtzion, 'Patterns of Islamization in West Africa', in Daniel F. McCall and Norman R. Bennett (eds), *Aspects of West African Islam* (Boston, Mass., 1971) pp. 31–9.

41. Above, pp. 43, 39.

42. C. C. Wrigley, quoted by Gavin Williams, 'The Social Stratification of

a Neo-Colonial Economy: Western Nigeria', in Christopher Allen and R. W. Johnson (eds), *African Perspectives* (Cambridge: Cambridge University Press, 1970) p. 247.

43. J. S. Eades, *The Yoruba Today* (Cambridge: Cambridge University Press, 1980) p. 78. Generally, see Christopher Beer, *The Politics of Peasant Groups in Western Nigeria* (Ibadan: Ibadan University Press, 1976).

44. See Sklar, *Nigerian Parties*, p. 478; Kenneth W. J. Post and George D. Jenkins, *The Price of Liberty* (Cambridge: Cambridge University Press, 1973) passim.

45. See Allan Hoben, *Land Tenure among the Amhara of Ethiopia* (Chicago: University of Chicago, 1973).

46. John M. Cohen and Dov Weintraub, *Land and Peasants in Imperial Ethiopia* (Van Gorcum, 1975).

47. Quoted in Patrick Gilkes, *The Dying Lion: Feudalism and Modernization in Ethiopia* (London: Friedmann, 1975) p. 70.

48. Hoben, *Land Tenure*, p. 231. See also Gilkes, *Dying Lion*, pp. 184–5.

49. Michael Stahl, *Ethiopia: Political Contradictions in Agricultural Development* (Uppsala: Political Science Association, 1974) passim; Gilkes, *Dying Lion*, ch. 4.

50. René Lefort, *Ethiopie: la révolution hérétique* (Paris: Maspero, 1981) pp. 146–65; Michael Stahl, *New Seeds in Old Soil: a Study of the Land Reform Process in Western Wollega, Ethiopia 1975–76* (Uppsala: Scandinavian Institute of African Studies, 1977); John M. Cohen, 'Green Revolution in Ethiopia', in James R. Scarritt (ed.), *Analyzing Political Change in Africa* (Boulder: Westview, 1980) pp. 134–7.

51. Quoted by Lefort, *Ethiopie*, p. 148, from a paper by Allan Hoben which I have not seen. I have retranslated the passage from the French.

52. Lefort, *Ethiopie*, pp. 168–9, 340–8; Fred Halliday and Maxine Molyneux, *The Ethiopian Revolution* (London: Verso, 1981) p. 109.

53. Jack Goody, 'Rice-Burning and the Green Revolution in Northern Ghana', *Journal of Development Studies*, XVI (1979–80) 151. See also Andrew Shepherd, 'Agrarian Change in Northern Ghana', in Judith Heyer and others (eds), *Rural Development in Tropical Africa* (London: Macmillan, 1981) pp. 168–92.

54. *West Africa*, 23 November 1981, p. 2,756; G. Nicolas, '"Guerre sainte" à Kano', *Politique africaine*, I, 4 (Novembre 1981) 47–70.

55. This account is based on Catherine E. Robins, '"Tukutendereza": a Study of Social Change and Sectarian Withdrawal in the "Balokole" Revival of Uganda', Ph.D. thesis, Columbia University, 1975.

56. Quoted in ibid., p. 447.

57. E. J. Hobsbawm and George Rude, *Captain Swing* (London: Lawrence & Wishart, 1969).

58. This account is based on Stanley R. Barrett, *The Rise and Fall of an African Utopia* (Waterloo, Ontario: Wilfrid Laurier University Press, 1977). See also Adrian Hastings, *A History of African Christianity 1950–1975* (Cambridge: Cambridge University Press, 1979) p. 122.

59. Paul M. Lubeck, 'Unions, Workers and Consciousness in Kano, Nigeria: a View from Below', in Richard Sandbrook and Robin Cohen

(eds), *The Development of an African Working Class* (London: Longman, 1975) pp. 139–60; idem, 'Labour in Kano since the Petroleum Boom', *Review of African Political Economy*, XIII (May 1978) 37–46; idem, 'Conscience de classe et nationalisme islamique à Kano', *Politique africaine*, I, 4 (Novembre 1981) 31–46; idem, 'Early Industrialization and Social Class Formation among Factory Workers in Kano, Nigeria', Ph.D. thesis, Northwestern University, 1975.

CHAPTER 4: Capitalists and Politicians

1. Alexander Gerschenkron, *Economic Backwardness in Historical Perspective* (Cambridge, Mass.: Harvard University Press, 1962).
2. In Dakar, from the 1930s. See A. Hauser, 'Les Industries de transformation de la région de Dakar', in P. Mercier, L. Massé and A. Hauser, *L'Agglomération dakaroise* (reprinted, Amsterdam: Swets and Zeitlinger, 1970) p. 69.
3. Peter Kilby, *Industrialization in an Open Economy: Nigeria 1945–1966* (Cambridge: Cambridge University Press, 1969) ch. 3; Nicola Swainson, *The Development of Corporate Capitalism in Kenya 1918–77* (London: Heinemann, 1980) ch. 3.
4. Carl Liedholm, 'The Influence of Colonial Policy on the Growth and Development of Nigeria's Industrial Sector', in Carl K. Eicher and Carl Liedholm (eds), *Growth and Development of the Nigerian Economy* ([East Lansing:] Michigan State University Press, 1970) p. 54.
5. Sara S. Berry and Carl Liedholm, 'Performance of the Nigerian Economy, 1950–1962', in ibid., p. 74.
6. S. O. Olayide (ed.), *Economic Survey of Nigeria (1960–1975)* (Ibadan: Aromolaran Publishing Company Limited, 1976) p. 13.
7. *West Africa*, 27 July 1981, p. 1,718, and 16 November 1981, p. 2,746; *African Business*, February 1982, p. 30.
8. See, e.g., Swainson, *Development*, passim; Paul T. Kennedy, *Ghanaian Businessmen: from Artisan to Capitalist Entrepreneur in a Dependent Economy* (München: Weltforum Verlag, 1980) passim.
9. R. H. Green, 'Foreign Direct Investment and African Political Economy', in Adebayo Adedeji (ed.), *Indigenization of African Economies* (London: Hutchinson, 1981) p. 341.
10. E.g. J. R. Harris, 'Nigerian Entrepreneurship in Industry', in Eicher and Liedholm, *Growth*, p. 312.
11. Kennedy, *Businessmen*, p. 89; Mary P. Rowe, 'Indigenous Industrial Entrepreneurship in Lagos, Nigeria', Ph.D. thesis, Columbia University, 1971, p. 207.
12. Gillian P. Hart, *Some Socio-Economic Aspects of African Entrepreneurship, with Particular Reference to the Transkei and Ciskei* (Institute of Social and Economic Research, Rhodes University, Grahamstown: Occasional Paper No. 16, 1972) pp. 68–71; Peter Marris and Anthony Somerset, *African Businessmen: a Study of Entrepreneurship and Development in Kenya* (London: Routledge & Kegan Paul, 1971) pp. 60–1; Andrew A. Beveridge and Anthony R. Oberschall, *African Businessmen and*

Development in Zambia (Princeton: Princeton University Press, 1979) pp. 122–3; Rowe, 'Indigenous Entrepreneurship', pp. 164, 219.

13.   Peter Kilby, *African Enterprise: the Nigerian Bread Industry* (Stanford: Hoover Institution, 1965) pp. 91–3, 98–101.

14.   Harris in Eicher and Liedholm, *Growth*, p. 312.

15.   Leo Kuper, *An African Bourgeoisie: Race, Class, and Politics in South Africa* (New Haven: Yale University Press, 1965) p. 266.

16.   Beveridge and Oberschall, *Businessmen*, pp. 129–30.

17.   John R. Harris, 'Nigerian Enterprise in the Printing Industry', *Nigerian Journal of Economic and Social Studies*, X (1968) 221; Rowe, 'Indigenous Entrepreneurship', p. 159.

18.   Rowe, 'Indigenous Entrepreneurship', pp. 217–24.

19.   Taiwo D. A. Idemudia, 'An Inquiry into the Performance of Nigerian Indigenous Entrepreneurs', Ph.D. thesis, State University of New York at Buffalo, 1978, pp. 143, 139, 192.

20.   Anthony Kirk-Greene and Douglas Rimmer, *Nigeria since 1970* (London: Hodder & Stoughton, 1981) p. 57; Kennedy, *Businessmen*, p. 20; Carolyn L. Baylies, 'Class Formation and the State in Zambia', Ph.D. thesis, University of Wisconsin, 1978, p. 968; Swainson, *Development*, p. 191.

21.   Rowe, 'Indigenous Entrepreneurship', p. 182; Sayre P. Schatz, *Nigerian Capitalism* (Berkeley: University of California, 1977) ch. 4; Marris and Somerset, *Businessmen*, ch. 8; Ikwuakam Diaku, 'A Capital Surplus Illusion: the Nigerian Case Revisited', *Nigerian Journal of Economic and Social Studies*, XIV (1972) 135–46; Idemudia, 'Inquiry', p. 8.

22.   Harris in Eicher and Liedholm, *Growth*, pp. 315–17; Beveridge and Oberschall, *Businessmen*, pp. 126–9; Kennedy, *Businessmen*, p. 49; Idemudia, 'Inquiry', pp. 134–5, 156.

23.   Samir Amin, *Le Développement du capitalisme en Côte d'Ivoire* (Paris: Editions de Minuit, 1967) pp. 279–80, 305.

24.   Fernand Braudel, *The Mediterranean and the Mediterranean World in the Age of Philip II*, trans. S. Reynolds, 2 vols (London: Collins, 1972–3) vol. II, p. 729.

25.   Antony G. Hopkins, 'Property Rights and Empire Building: Britain's Annexation of Lagos, 1861', *Journal of Economic History*, XL (1980) 777–98; Joe G. Nwaorgu, 'Urban Land Ownership in Nigeria: an Analytical Study of Attitudes and Policies in Enugu and Jos', Ph.D. thesis, Cambridge University, 1979.

26.   Nici Nelson, 'How Women and Men get by: the Sexual Division of Labour in the Informal Sector of a Nairobi Squatter Settlement', in Ray Bromley and Chris Gerry (eds), *Casual Work and Poverty in Third World Cities* (Chichester: John Wiley, 1979) p. 289.

27.   Andrew Hake, *African Metropolis: Nairobi's Self-Help City* ([London] Sussex University Press, 1977) p. 75.

28.   Peter C. Garlick, *African Traders and Economic Development in Ghana* (Oxford: Clarendon, 1971) p. 146.

29.   Ibid., pp. 97, 149; Keith Hart, 'Swindler or Public Benefactor? – the Entrepreneur in his Community', in Jack Goody (ed.), *Changing Social*

Structure in Ghana (London: International African Institute, 1975) p. 17.

30. Kennedy, *Businessmen*, pp. 107–10; Beveridge and Oberschall, *Businessmen*, pp. 294–5.
31. E. O. Akeredolu-Ale, 'A Sociohistorical Study of the Development of Entrepreneurship among the Ijebu of Western Nigeria', *African Studies Review*, XVI (1973) 347–64; Peter C. Garlick, 'The Development of Kwahu Business Enterprise in Ghana since 1874', *Journal of African History*, VIII (1967) 463–80; Keith Hart, 'Small-Scale Entrepreneurs in Ghana and Development Planning', *Journal of Development Studies*, VI, 4 (July 1970) 104–20.
32. E. O. Akeredolu-Ale, *The Underdevelopment of Indigenous Entrepreneurship in Nigeria* (Ibadan: Ibadan University Press, 1975) pp. 77–84.
33. For an excellent survey of the literature on management, see Peter Kilby (ed.), *Entrepreneurship and Economic Development* (New York: Free Press, 1971) ch. 1.
34. Sidney Pollard, *The Genesis of Modern Management* (London: Edward Arnold, 1965) pp. 59–60, 165.
35. Morris D. Morris, *The Emergence of an Industrial Labor Force in India* (Berkeley: University of California, 1965) passim; Kang Chao, *The Development of Cotton Textile Production in China* (Cambridge, Mass.: Harvard University Press, 1977) pp. 153–4.
36. Johannes Hirschmeier and Tsunehiko Yui, *The Development of Japanese Business, 1600–1973* (London: George Allen & Unwin, 1975) p. 199; James C. Abegglen, *The Japanese Factory* (reprinted, Bombay: Asia Publishing House, 1959) p. 75.
37. Paul M. Lubeck, 'Early Industrialization and Social Class Formation among Factory Workers in Kano, Nigeria', Ph.D. thesis, Northwestern University, 1975, p. 90; idem, 'Labour in Kano since the Petroleum Boom', *Review of African Political Economy*, XIII (May 1978), 44; Margaret Peil, *The Ghanaian Factory Worker* (Cambridge University Press, 1972) pp. 90, 95, 98.
38. Kilby, *Entrepreneurship*, pp. 38–40.
39. Marris and Somerset, *Businessmen*, pp. 107–16; Hart, *Socio-Economic Aspects*, pp. 166–7; Beveridge and Oberschall, *Businessmen*, pp. 150–1.
40. Ronald Dore, *British Factory, Japanese Factory: the Origins of National Diversity in Industrial Relations* (London: George Allen & Unwin, 1973) chs 14 and 15.
41. Ibid., p. 395.
42. Peil, *Ghanaian Worker*; Adrian J. Peace, *Choice, Class and Conflict: a Study of Southern Nigerian Factory Workers* (Brighton: Harvester Press, 1979).
43. Steven W. Langdon, *Multinational Corporations in the Political Economy of Kenya* (London: Macmillan, 1981) pp. 142–4; Robin Cohen, *Labour and Politics in Nigeria 1945–71* (London: Heinemann, 1974) ch 4; Dorothy Remy, 'Economic Security and Industrial Unionism: a Nigerian Case Study', in Richard Sandbrook and Robin Cohen (eds), *The Development of an African Working Class* (London: Longman, 1975) pp. 161–77.
44. See esp. Peace, *Choice*.
45. Kennedy, *Businessmen*, p. 114; Hart, *Socio-Economic Aspects*, p. 157.

46. Marris and Somerset, *Businessmen*, p. 124.
47. Rowe, 'Indigenous Entrepreneurship', p. 81.
48. Samir Amin, *Le Monde des affaires sénégalais* (Paris: Editions de Minuit, 1969) p. 181.
49. Garlick, *Traders*, p. 93.
50. Rowe, 'Indigenous Entrepreneurship', p. 181.
51. Ahmed Beita Yusuf, 'Capital Formation and Management among the Muslim Hausa Traders of Kano, Nigeria', *Africa*, XLV (1975) 181.
52. Paul E. Lovejoy, 'The Wholesale Kola Trade of Kano',*African Urban Notes*, V (1970) 138.
53. Idemudia, 'Inquiry', pp. 170, 206.
54. Akeredolu-Ale, *Underdevelopment*, p. 58; Langdon, *Multinational Corporations*, ch. 4; Richard Eglin, 'The Oligopolistic Structure and Competitive Characteristics of Direct Foreign Investment in Kenya's Manufacturing Sector', in Raphael Kaplinsky (ed.), *Readings on the Multinational Corporation in Kenya* (Nairobi: Oxford University Press, 1978) p. 132; Marris and Somerset, *Businessmen*, pp. 13–14; Schatz, *Capitalism*, pp. 113–14; Paul Kennedy, 'Indigenous Capitalism in Ghana', *Review of African Political Economy*, VIII (January 1977) 35; Rowe, 'Indigenous Entrepreneurship', p. 191.
55. Kennedy, 'Indigenous Capitalism', p. 35.
56. Paul Kennedy, 'African Businessmen and Foreign Capital: Collaboration or Conflict?', *African Affairs*, LXXVI (1977) 177–94.
57. *The Weekly Review*, 10 April 1981, p. 21, and 12 March 1982, p. 5.
58. *Nigeria Newsletter*, 25 May 1981.
59. D. K. Fieldhouse, *Unilever Overseas: the Anatomy of a Multinational, 1895–1965* (London: Croom Helm, 1978) pp. 575, 313, 487.
60. *African Business*, December 1979, p. 14.
61. E. Ayeh-Kumi, quoted in Tony Killick, *Development Economics in Action: a Study of Economic Policies in Ghana* (London: Heinemann, 1978) p. 60 n. 27.
62. Ibid., p. 155.
63. Julius K. Nyerere, 'The Arusha Declaration Ten Years After' (1977), in Andrew Coulson (ed.), *African Socialism in Practice: the Tanzanian Experience* (Nottingham: Spokesman, 1979) p. 46. For studies of the growth of rural capitalism, see Lionel Cliffe and others (eds), *Rural Cooperation in Tanzania* (Dar es Salaam: Tanzania Publishing House, 1975).
64. The most recent study, with bibliography, is Andrew Coulson, *Tanzania: a Political Economy* (Oxford: Clarendon, 1982).
65. Adhu Awiti, 'Lutte des classes dans la société rurale de la Tanzanie: une étude de cas de Ismani-Iringa', in Samir Amin (ed.), *L'Agriculture africaine et le capitalisme* (Paris: Anthropos, 1975) p. 275; Jannik Boesen and A. T. Mohele, *The 'Success Story' of Peasant Tobacco Production in Tanzania* (Uppsala: Scandinavian Institute of African Studies, 1979) chs 3 and 4; Goran Hyden, *Beyond Ujamaa in Tanzania* (London: Heinemann, 1980) pp. 102–4.
66. Information from several recent students of rural Tanzania.
67. Nyerere in Coulson, *African Socialism*, pp. 43–4.

68. Quoted in René Lemarchand, 'The Politics of Penury in Rural Zaire: the View from Bandundu', in Guy Gran (ed.), *Zaire: the Political Economy of Underdevelopment* (New York: Praeger, 1979) pp. 248–9.

69. Michael G. Schatzberg, *Politics and Class in Zaire* (New York: Africana Publishing Company, 1980) p. 168.

70. Ibid., ch. 7; idem, 'The State and the Economy: the "Radicalization of the Revolution" in Mobutu's Zaire', *Canadian Journal of African Studies*, XIV (1980) 239–57; Edward Kannyo, 'Political Power and Class-Formation in Zaire: the "Zairianization Measures", 1973–1975', Ph.D. thesis, Yale University, 1979.

71. *Le Monde diplomatique*, Novembre 1981, p. 21. For more productive capitalism, see Janet MacGaffey, 'Business and Class Formation in Kisangani', duplicated paper, 'Colloquy on Enterprises in Africa', Paris, December 1981.

72. Baylies, 'Class Formation', esp. p. 860.

73. Kadallah Khafre, 'Towards a Political Economy of Liberia', *Review of African Political Economy*, XII (May 1978) 105; The Official Papers of William V. S. Tubman . . . 1960–1967 (London: Longman, 1968) pp. 381–4; Wilton Sankawulo, *In the Cause of the People: an Interpretation of President Tolbert's Philosophy of Humanistic Capitalism* (Monrovia: Ministry of Information, Cultural Affairs and Tourism, n.d.) pp. 6–7; *African Business*, March 1982, p. 21.

74. *Fraternité hebdo* (Abidjan), 4 Septembre 1981, p. 4.

75. Claude de Miras, 'De la Bourgeoisie d'état à l'avènement d'un milieu d'entrepreneurs ivoiriens?', duplicated paper, 'Colloquy on Enterprises in Africa', Paris, December 1981.

76. Philippe Lena, 'Le Problème de la main-d'oeuvre en zone pionnière, quelques points de repère', *Cahiers du CIRES,* XXIII (Décembre 1979) 97.

77. Michael A. Cohen, *Urban Policy and Political Conflict in Africa: a Study of the Ivory Coast* (Chicago: University of Chicago, 1974) pp. 43, 66.

78. Henrik S. Marcussen and Jens E. Torp, 'The Ivory Coast – Towards Self-Centered Development?' in Kirsten Worm (ed.), *Industrialization, Development and the Demands for a New International Economic Order* (Copenhagen: Samfundsvidenskabeligt Forlag, 1978) p. 173; *Fraternité matin* (Abidjan), 14 Septembre 1981.

79. Quoted in de Miras, 'De la Bourgeoisie'.

80. Quoted in *Le Monde diplomatique*, Novembre 1981, p. 17.

81. Schatz, *Capitalism*, pp. 3–4.

82. See *Nigeria Newsletter*, April and May 1981; *West Africa*, 28 September 1981, p. 2,278, and 2 November 1981, p. 2,605; *African Business*, May 1982, p. 36.

83. Arthur Hazlewood, *The Economy of Kenya: the Kenyatta Era* (Oxford: Oxford University Press, 1979) pp. 32–4, 91; Swainson, *Development*, pp. 199–200, 208–11.

84. *The Weekly Review*, 12 March 1982, p. 5.

85. Roger van Zwanenberg, 'Neocolonialism and the Origin of the National Bourgeoisie in Kenya', *Journal of Eastern African Research and Development*, IV (1974) 171–3; Lionel Cliffe and Peter Lawrence, 'Editorial', *Review of African Political Economy*, VIII (January 1977) 3–4.

86.   *West Africa*, 27 April 1981, p. 929; Paul Collins, 'Public Policy and the Development of Indigenous Capitalism: the Nigerian Experience', *Journal of Commonwealth and Comparative Politics*, XV (1977) p. 142.
87.   Ankie Hoogvelt, 'Indigenisation and Foreign Capital: Industrialisation in Nigeria', *Review of African Political Economy*, XIV (January 1979) 56–68; idem, 'Indigenization and Technological Dependency', *Development and Change*, XI (1980) 257–72.
88.   O. F. Onoge, 'The Indigenisation Decree and Economic Independence: Another Case of Bourgeois Utopianism', in Nigerian Economic Society, *Nigeria's Indigenisation Policy: Proceedings of the November 1974 Symposium* (Ibadan, n.d.) p. 64.
89.   Colin Leys, 'Capital Accumulation, Class Formation and Dependency – the Significance of the Kenyan Case', *Socialist Register* (1978) pp. 262–3; Robert Brenner, 'Agrarian Class Structure and Economic Development', *Past and Present*, 70 (February 1976) 30–75.

Further Reading

Akeredolu-Ale, E. O., *The Underdevelopment of Indigenous Entrepreneurship in Nigeria* (Ibadan: Ibadan University Press, 1975).

Amin, Samir, *Le Développement du capitalisme en Côte d'Ivoire* (Paris: Editions de Minuit, 1967).

Amin, Samir, *Le Monde des affaires sénégalais* (Paris: Editions de Minuit, 1969).

Amin, Samir (ed.), *L'Agriculture africaine et le capitalisme* (Paris: Anthropos, 1975).

Amselle, Jean-Loup, *Les Négociants de la savane: histoire et organisation sociale des Kooroko (Mali)* (Paris: Anthropos, 1977).

Baier, Stephen, *An Economic History of Central Niger* (Oxford: Clarendon, 1980).

Beer, Christopher, *The Politics of Peasant Groups in Western Nigeria* (Ibadan: Ibadan University Press, 1976).

Beveridge, Andrew A., and Oberschall, Anthony R., *African Businessmen and Development in Zambia* (Princeton: Princeton University Press, 1979).

Bundy, Colin, *The Rise and Fall of the South African Peasantry* (London: Heinemann, 1979).

Coulson, Andrew, *Tanzania: a Political Economy* (Oxford: Clarendon, 1982).

Garlick, Peter C., *African Traders and Economic Development in Ghana* (Oxford: Clarendon, 1971)

Gran, Guy (ed.), *Zaire: the Political Economy of Underdevelopment* (New York: Praeger, 1979).

Halliday, Fred, and Molyneux, Maxine, *The Ethiopian Revolution* (London: Verso, 1981).

Hart, Gillian P., *Some Socio-Economic Aspects of African Entrepreneurship, with Particular Reference to the Transkei and Ciskei* (Institute of Social and Economic Research, Rhodes University, Grahamstown, Occasional Paper No. 16, Grahamstown, 1972).

Heyer, Judith, and others (ed.), *Rural Development in Tropical Africa* (London: Macmillan, 1981).

Hill, Polly, *The Gold Coast Cocoa Farmer* (London: Oxford University Press, 1956).

Hill, Polly, *The Migrant Cocoa-Farmers of Southern Ghana* (Cambridge: Cambridge University Press, 1963).

Hoogvelt, Ankie, 'Indigenization and Foreign Capital: Industrialization in Nigeria', *Review of African Political Economy*, XIV (January 1979) 56–68.

Hoogvelt, Ankie, 'Indigenization and Technological Dependency', *Development and Change*, XI (1980) 257–72.

Hopkins, A. G., *An Economic History of West Africa* (London: Longman, 1973).

Iliffe, John, *A Modern History of Tanganyika* (Cambridge: Cambridge University Press, 1979).

Kennedy, Paul T., *Ghanaian Businessmen: from Artisan to Capitalist Entrepreneur in a Dependent Economy* (München: Weltforum Verlag, 1980).

Kilby, Peter, *African Enterprise: the Nigerian Bread Industry* (Stanford: Hoover Institution, 1965).

Kilby, Peter, *Industrialization in an Open Economy: Nigeria 1945–1966* (Cambridge: Cambridge University Press, 1969).

Killick, Tony, *Development Economics in Action: a Study of Economic Policies in Ghana* (London: Heinemann, 1978).

Kitching, Gavin, *Class and Economic Change in Kenya: the Making of an African Petite Bourgeoisie 1905–1970* (New Haven: Yale University Press, 1980).

Lefort, René, *Ethiopie: la révolution hérétique* (Paris: Maspero, 1981).

Leys, Colin, 'Capital Accumulation, Class Formation and Dependency – the Significance of the Kenyan Case', *Socialist Register* (1978) pp. 241–66.

Long, Norman, *Social Change and the Individual* (Manchester: Manchester University Press, 1968).

Lubeck, Paul M. (ed.), *The African Bourgeoisie: the Development of Capitalism in the Ivory Coast, Kenya, and Nigeria* (forthcoming).

Mafeje, A., *Agrarian Revolution and the Land Question in Buganda* (Institute of Social Studies, The Hague: Occasional Paper No. 32, 1973).

Marris, Peter, and Somerset, Anthony, *African Businessmen: a Study of Entrepreneurship and Development in Kenya* (London: Routledge & Kegan Paul, 1971).

Mischlich, A., *Ueber die Kulturen im Mittel-Sudan* (Berlin: Reimer, 1942).

Monteil, Charles, *Monographie de Djénné: cercle et ville* (Tulle: Mazeyrie, 1903).

Munslow, Barry, 'Zimbabwe's Emerging African Bourgeoisie', *Review of African Political Economy*, XIX (September 1980) 63–9.

Parkin, David J., *Palms, Wine, and Witnesses: Public Spirit and Private Gain in an African Farming Community* (London: Intertext, 1972).

Piault, Colette (ed.), *Prophétisme et thérapeutique: Albert Atcho et la communauté de Bregbo* (Paris: Hermann, 1975).

Rey, Pierre-Philippe, *Les Alliances de classes* (Paris: Maspero, 1973).

Rey, Pierre-Philippe, *Colonialisme, néo-colonialisme et transition au capitalisme: exemple de la 'Comilog' au Congo-Brazzaville* (Paris: Maspero, 1971).

Richards, Audrey I., and others (ed.), *Subsistence to Commercial Farming in Present-Day Buganda* (Cambridge: Cambridge University Press, 1973).

Robertson, A. F., 'Abusa: the Structural History of an Economic Contract', *Journal of Development Studies*, forthcoming.

Sandbrook, Richard, and Cohen, Robin (eds), *The Development of an African Working Class* (London: Longman, 1975).

Schatz, Sayre P., *Nigerian Capitalism* (Berkeley: University of California, 1977).

Shea, Philip J., 'Economies of Scale and the Indigo Dyeing Industry of Precolonial Kano', *Kano Studies*, NS, I, 2 (1974–7) 55–61.

Swainson, Nicola, *The Development of Corporate Capitalism in Kenya 1918–77* (London: Heinemann, 1980).

Weinrich, A. K. H., *African Farmers in Rhodesia: Old and New Peasant Communities in Karangaland* (London: Oxford University Press, 1975).

Wilks, Ivor, 'The Golden Stool and the Elephant Tail: an Essay on Wealth in Asante', *Research in Economic Anthropology*, II (1979) 1–36.

Index